INTRODUCTION

Marijuana has its advantages and disadvantages, depending on which political and religious party you're talking to. Bottom line is that marijuana is a plant grown from the grown and produced by our very own Mother Nature. If abused, misused or overused, it can be catastrophic to one's body, mind and cognition abilities; however, when used appropriately, it can cure many ailments such as fear or nervousness, anorexia, pain, nausea and vomiting, just t name a few.

Indians (meaning those native to the Americas, not the country India) have used cannabis for medicinal purposes for centuries. They used it in cooking, drinking, and even some ointments to be rubbed periodically on insect bites or stings, as well as cuts caused from every-day interaction with mother nature. It's important to remember, here that marijuana is not a harmful, intoxicating drug that injures our bodies, but can be used for many purposes to help it. There are several books and sites on nature's medicine that give recipes for these medicines, which are incredibly helpful if you can gain access to the said ingredients.

Some states in the U.S.A. have finally given in to allowing medical marijuana; however, they have also created loopholes in those allowances that can get one in a fair amount of legal trouble if caught with over a certain amount of it. There are many ideas and conspiracy theories as to why this is. Some think it is because the government cannot figure out how to control its growth and manufacturing like they do with alcohol and tobacco, while others have been made to believe that it truly is harmful to the body. Don't misunderstand, there are some negative effects of marijuana when used for recreation; namely, one tends to become less coherent and quick to respond, overeating, as well as extreme fatigue. We live in a fast-pa~~~ world, so using marijuana as a recreational drug can somewhat dampen the effects of the fast merry-go-round of lif

Due to the legal complications of marijuana use, it is hard to opening speak about such matters to government offic however, we the people have the right to learn the true nature of Nature's Gifts and medicines and fight for the righ them. Statistically, marijuana is not nearly as harmful to our society as alcohol and tobacco, in which those 2 drugs t effect the public when consumed individually.

Our society has come a long way so far in somewhat legalizing the use of medical marijuana, and it is up to us to cor onto this road of progression as it is our right, nay, our duty, as American citizens to enforce societal change.

RECIPES

Marijuana Mustard Crusted Halibut

Marijuana Salad Dressing

Marijuana Lemon Pepper Dressing

Cilantro Marijuana Marinade

Marijuana Marinade

Béarnaise Sauce

Marijuana Spinach

Marijuana Asparagus With Sesame Seeds

Sautéed Marijuana Zucchini

Marijuana Garlic And Red Wine Filet Mignon

Marijuana Chicken Cordon Bleu

Marijuana Grilled Swordfish

Homemade High Hummus

Black Bean Buds Hummus

Marijuana Cheezy Margherita Pizza

Cannibutter

Marijuana Strawberry Banana Pancakes

Canni French Toast

Marijuana Coffee Cake

Marijuana Guacamole

"Home Grown" Marijuana Homemade Mashed Potatoes

Marijuana Butternut Squash Soup

Marijuana Cinnamon Rolls

Marijuana Sprinkle Brownies

Cannabis Crispy Treats

Cannadian Canna Pecan Pie

Chocolate Nut Canna Bites

Citrus Canna Bread

Marijuana Pot Wings

Mary's Mashed Pot Tatoes

Marijuana Bud Broccoli Cassarole

Marijuana Cheesy-Maccaroni-N- Treez

Marijuana High Stir-Fry

Ganja Peanut Butter Cookies

Late Night Marijuana Munchie Pancakes

Kidney Bean And Marijuana Mushroom Veggie Burger

Black Bean Marijuana Veggie Burgers

Marijuana Chili Con Carne

Marijuana Balsamic Vinaigrette

Marijuana Meat Loaf

Marijuana Spaghetti

Marijuana Baked Salmon

Marijuana Banana Bread

Marijuana Mayonnaise

Ganja Cheesecake

Cannabis Butter

Marijuana Milk

Granola Infused With Marijuana

Marijuana Stoney Spaghetti Sauce

Marijuana Brownies With Walnuts

Marijuana Tea

Marijuana Lobster Rolls

Marijuana Lifesaver Pizza

Marijuana Knoll Guacamole

Apple Pie With Marijuana

Marijuana Pepper And Artichoke Dip

Marijuana Chili

Marijuana Turkey Stuffing

Marijuana Crab Stuff Mushrooms

Marijuana Alfredo Pasta Sauce

Marijuana Potato And Olive Oil Soup

Marijuana Fried Butter Balls

Marijuana Cilantro And Sun Dried Tomato Pesto

Marijuana Chicken Pot Pie

Marijuana Tomato Basil Pasta

Marijuana Grilled Macadamia Crusted Tuna With Papaya Salsa

Marijuana Grilled Salmon

Marijuana Maple Salmon

Marijuana Fish Tacos

Marijuana Baked Tilapia

Marijuana Hash Brown Casserole

Marijuana Reuben Sandwich

Marijuana Barbecued Beef Sandwiches

Marijuana Creamy Basil Chicken Pasta

Marijuana Garlic Basil Grilled Shrimp Pasta

Marijuana Bloody Mari

Marijuana Screwdriver

Marijuana Jello Shots

Marijuana Iced Coffee

Marijuana Cupcakes

Marijuana Appie Pecan Galaxy Cake
Canna Creamy Potato Salad
Ganja Garilc Mashed Potatoes
Sativa Shrimp Burritos
Canna Cajun Seafood Pasta
Mexican Marijuana Chicken Corn Chowder
Marijuana Lasagna
Marijuana Mac N' Cheese
Marijuana Scrambler
Marijuana Breakfast Baked Burritos
Vegetarian Marijuana Chili
Marijuana Cinnamon Pecan Sandies
Marijuana Truffles
Marijuana Banana Blueberry Smoothie
Marijuana Chocolate Milkshake
Marijuana Oatmeal Cookies
Marijuana Chocolate Pudding
Chocolate Chip Cannabutter Bar
Marijuana Olivada
Marijuana Flat Bread
Marijuana Tiramisu Milk Shake
Marijuana Cinnamon Coffee Cake
Marijuana Red Velvet Cupcakes
Marijuana Sloppy Joe Sandwiches
Marijuana Lemon Bread
Marijuana Sugar Cookies

Recipes: MARIJUANA EDIBLES

Serving 4

Marijuana Mustard Cursted Halibut

INGREDIENTS

1. 1 teaspoon whole grain mustard
2. 1 teaspoon chopped fresh thyme
3. 1 tablespoon chopped fresh oregano
4. 1 teaspoon water
5. 2 tablespoons Marijuana butter
6. 1 teaspoon chopped fresh rosemary
7. 6 oz center cut halibut steak
8. ½ teaspoon freshly ground black pepper

DIRECTIONS

- ❖ Preheat oven to 350°F. (175°C)
- ❖ Collect mustard, thyme, oregano, rosemary, pepper, water into a small size bowl, mix all together and blend well to make a paste.
- ❖ Butter an oven proof baking dish. Place halibut in the dish and spread with the mustard herb paste. Bake for about 15 – 20 minutes, or until fish flakes easily with a fork.

Recipes: MARIJUANA EDIBLES

Serving 4

Marijuana Breakfast Baked Burritos

INGREDIENTS

1. 4 eggs
2. 2 tablespoons Marijuana butter
3. 6 ounces bacon
4. 3/8 (16 ounce) can refried beans
5. 4 (10 inch) flour tortillas
6. 3 ounces shredded Cheddar cheese

DIRECTIONS

- Collect bacon in a large, deep skillet. Cook over medium high heat until evenly brown. Drain, and set aside. Wrap the tortillas in foil and warm in the oven.
- Fry eggs in a greased skillet until firm over Marijuana butter. In a small sauce pan heat the refried beans.
- Top each tortilla with refried beans, 2 strips of bacon, 1 egg and a little cheese. Roll tortillas into burritos and serve.

Recipes: MARIJUANA EDIBLES

Serving	16

Vegetarian Marijuana Chili

INGREDIENTS

1. 2 tablespoon Marijuana butter
2. 3 cloves garlic, minced
3. 1 cup chopped onion
4. 1 cup chopped carrots
5. 1 cup chopped green bell pepper
6. 1 cup chopped red bell pepper
7. 2 tablespoons chili powder
8. 1 ½ cups chopped fresh mushrooms
9. 1 (28 ounce) can whole peeled tomatoes with liquid, chopped
10. 1 (15 ounce) can black beans, undrained
11. 1 (15 ounce) can kidney beans, undrained
12. 1 (15 ounce) can pinto beans, undrained
13. 1 tablespoon cumin
14. 1 ½ tablespoons dried oregano
15. 1 ½ tablespoons dried basil
16. ½ tablespoon garlic powder

DIRECTIONS

❖ Heat Marijuana butter in a large pot over medium heat, until melt. Add garlic, onion, carrots in the pot and cook for few minutes or until tender.

❖ add in green bell pepper and red bell pepper. Season with chili powder. Keep cooking for another 5 minutes, or until peppers are tender.

❖ Add mushrooms and for few seconds. Stir in tomatoes with liquid, black beans with liquid, kidney beans with liquid, and pinto beans with liquid. Season with cumin, oregano, basil, and garlic powder. Allow to boil. Reduce heat to medium, cover, and cook for 20 minutes, stirring occasionally.

Recipes: MARIJUANA EDIBLES

Serving: 4

Marijuana Cinnamon Pecan Sandies

INGREDIENTS

1. 1 cup ground pecans
1. ½ cup sifted powdered sugar
2. 2 cups all purpose flour
3. ½ teaspoon baking powder
4. 1 tablespoon vanilla extract
2. 1 cup cannabutter
5. 1 cup natural brown sugar
6. 2 teaspoons cinnamon

DIRECTIONS

- Mix weed butter and sugar together in a mixing bowl until smooth. While mixing add in
- vanilla. Mix together flour and baking powder and gradually add it to your mixing bowl. Add the chopped pecans. Cover the dough and chill for 3 – 4 hours.
- Remove dough from refrigerator and roll it into golf sized balls before gently flattening them in your hand and placing them on an ungreased cookie sheet. Bake for about 20 minutes at 325°F or until slightly firm and golden. Remove from the oven and gently placing them on a cooling rack.
- Collect mix powdered sugar and cinnamon and then dust them with the mixture. Allow them to completely cool to avoid crumbling. Serve and enjoy.

Recipes: MARIJUANA EDIBLES

Marijuana Truffles

Serving 4

INGREDIENTS

1. 4 tablespoon CannaButter
2. 12 oz. Semi sweet chocolate morsels
3. 2 beaten egg yolks
4. ¾ cup super fine granulated sugar
5. 1 cup finely chopped walnuts, hazelnuts or almonds
6. $1/3$ cup liqueur (Kahlua)

DIRECTIONS

- Melt chocolate morsels in a fondue pot or double boiler, while steadily adding in the CannaButter. Once the butter has melted in, stirring constantly, add in sugar until it dissolves in the chocolate and butter.
- Remove pot from heat source and add 2 or 3 tablespoons to the beaten egg yolks to warm them up. Once you do this, add the egg yolks with the chocolate into the pot, mixing it in thoroughly.
- Mix in almonds and liqueur and pour onto a glass brownie pan. Place in the refrigerator to solidify. After 3 or 4 hours the truffles should be hardened and you may cut and form them to your desire shape. Store in the refrigerator or freezer. Serve and enjoy.

Recipes: MARIJUANA EDIBLES

Serving: 2

Marijuana Banana Blueberry Smoothie

INGREDIENTS

1. 1 cup canna milk
2. 1 sliced banana
3. 1 cup strawberry yogurt
4. 2 cups fresh blueberries

DIRECTIONS

- Collect all ingredients in a blender and blend until the consistency is smooth. Pour, serve and enjoy.

Recipes: MARIJUANA EDIBLES

Serving	2

Marijuana Chocolate Milkshake

INGREDIENTS

1. 3 scoops chocolate ice cream (medicated for extra potency)
2. ½ cup canna milk
3. chocolate syrup to taste

DIRECTIONS

❖ Collect all ingredients in a blender and blend until thoroughly blended and smooth consistency.

❖ For extra chocolate flavor and presentation, line the inside of a glass with chocolate syrup, pour the milkshake in and enjoy a tasty, medicinal treat.

Recipes: MARIJUANA EDIBLES

Serving: 6

Marijuana Oatmeal Cookies

INGREDIENTS

1. 4 cups uncooked regular oats
2. 1 ¾ cup ripe bananas, mashed up
3. ¾ cup cannabis infused olive oil
4. ⅓ cup honey
5. ¾ teaspoon salt
6. ½ cup nuts, chopped
7. ½ cup raisins (**Optional** replace with chocolate chips)

DIRECTIONS

- Per heat oven to 350°F.
- Mix together honey and oil in medium bowl, make sure is well blended. add in mashed bananas and salt, mix well. Add oats, nuts and raisins little by little, stirring in as you go.
- Drop by spoonfuls onto a cookie sheet and bake for about 20 – 25 minutes. Allow to cool for about 5 minutes and transfer from baking sheet to cooling rack. Serve warm.

Recipes: MARIJUANA EDIBLES

Serving	2

Marijuana Chocolate Pudding

INGREDIENTS

1. 2 cups cannabis milk
2. ½ cup frozen whipped topping, thawed
3. ½ teaspoon ground cinnamon
4. 1 box instant pudding mix, chocolate (14 oz)

DIRECTIONS

❖ Beat pudding mix add cannabis milk, cinnamon and whisk together for about two minutes.
❖ Stir in thawed whipped topping until thoroughly mixed. Refrigerate for about 30 minutes, and enjoy.

Recipes: MARIJUANA EDIBLES

Serving 4

Chocolate Chip Cannabutter Bar

INGREDIENTS

1. ½ teaspoon vanilla extract
2. 1/3 cups cannabutter
3. ¼ cup honey
4. 1/3 cup packed brown sugar
5. 1 cup crispy rice cereal
6. 2 – 3 tablespoons mini chocolate chips
7. 2 cups quick cooking oats (rolled oats don't work well)

DIRECTIONS

- Stir together oats and rice cereal in a large bowl and set aside.
- Heat butter, honey and brown sugar together, in a small pot, over medium high heat until it comes to a bubble. Reduce heat and cook for 2 minutes. Add in the vanilla and stir.
- Pour mixture over dry ingredients and mix well to moisten all ingredients. Pour everything into a lightly greased small 8 x 12 inch brownie pan and press out so that the mixture in the pan is about ¾ inch in thickness.
- Sprinkle mini chocolate chips on top and press down lightly. Allow everything to cool at room temperature for about two hours or until the chocolate chips are set before cutting into bars.
- Cut, wrap in parchment paper or plastic wrap, and store at room temperature in a cool dry place.

Serving	2 Cups

Marijuana Olivada

INGREDIENTS

1. 2 cloves fresh minced garlic
2. ¾ lbs. pitted olives
3. $\frac{1}{3}$ cup cannabis olive oil
4. Pepper to taste

DIRECTIONS

- ❖ Collect garlic, cannabis olive oil and olives into a blender, blend until smooth. If it comes out runny, add more olives. Put the paste in a pot or jar and stir in pepper.
- ❖ Put in a mason jar, pour a thin layer of cannabis olive oil on the top and store in the refrigerator. Spread on your favorite sourdough bread, add to egg dishes or even baked potatoes.

Recipes: MARIJUANA EDIBLES

Serving: ¾ Cup

Marijuana Salad Dressing

INGREDIENTS

1. ¼ cup canna oil
2. 1 teaspoons Dijon style mustard, smooth or grainy
3. 1 tablespoon flax seed oil
4. 2 tablespoon s + 1 teaspoon wine vinegar
5. ¼ cup olive oil

DIRECTIONS

- Whisk mustard into vinegar. Add both olive oil, and Marijuana oil in a thin stream, whisking constantly until oil is emulsified.
- Whisk in flax seed oil, and use immediately.

Recipes: MARIJUANA EDIBLES

Serving	¾ Cup

Marijuana Lemon Pepper Dressing

INGREDIENTS

6. ¼ cup Marijuana oil
7. 1 tablespoon wine vinegar
8. 1 dash stevia powder
9. 2 tablespoons fresh lemon juice
10. 1 clove garlic, minced
11. ¼ cup olive oil
12. 1 tablespoon flax seed oil
13. ¼ teaspoon salt
14. ½ teaspoon cracked black peppercorns

DIRECTIONS

❖ Collect all ingredients into small size bowl, and whisk vigorously until the mixture emulsifies.

Recipes: MARIJUANA EDIBLES

Serving — ¾ Cup

Cilantro Marijuana Marinade

INGREDIENTS

1. ¼ cup cup Marijuana oil
2. 3 cloves garlic, minced
3. 1 bunch cilantro, leaves only, finely chopped
4. juice of 1 lemon
5. ¼ cup olive oil
6. ¼ teaspoon freshly ground black pepper

DIRECTIONS

- Collect and mix all ingredients togrther in a medium size, until well mixed blended.
- Pour over food, and marinate overnight.

Recipes: MARIJUANA EDIBLES

Serving	¾ Cup

Marijuana Marinade

INGREDIENTS

1. ½ cup Marijuana oil
2. 3 teaspoons dried basil
3. 3 cups of olive oil
4. 1 red onion, sliced
5. 4 teaspoons freshly ground black pepper
6. 4 teaspoons paprika
7. 1 whole head garlic, cloves minced
8. 4 teaspoon Worcestershire sauce
9. 1 cup lemon juice
10. 1¼ cups red wine vinegar
11. 4 teaspoons salt
12. 4 teaspoons ground white pepper

DIRECTIONS

❖ Collect and mix all ingredients togrther in a medium size, until well mixed blended.
❖ Pour over food, and marinate overnight.

Recipes: MARIJUANA EDIBLES

Serving: ¾ Cup

Béarnaise Sauce

INGREDIENTS

1. ¼ cup Marijuana butter
2. 5 egg yolks, at room temperature
3. 2 tablespoons finely chopped shallots (or green onions)
4. fresh lemon juice to taste
5. 1 tablespoon finely chopped fresh tarragon (or 1 teaspoon dried tarragon)
6. 2 tablespoons white wine vinegar
7. 2 tablespoons dry white wine (or vermouth)
8. ¼ cup regular butter
9. pinch of salt
10. pinch of freshly ground black pepper

DIRECTIONS

- Collect shallots, tarragon, vinegar, and wine, into a small size saucepan, heat over medium high until boil, reduce to 1 tablespoon of liquid into a bowl and set aside.
- In another small bowl, whisk egg yolks and set aside.
- Heat water in a bowl, over low heat. Set bowl with the reduced liquid over hot water. Add about half the butter into bowl piece by piece, on the hot water, whisking the constantly with butter until melted.
- Add egg yolks slowly, bit by bit, whisking constantly. Add the remaining butter, and whisk until well amalgamated. Sauce should be warm and slightly thickened.
- Remove from heat and whisk in lemon juice, salt, and pepper. Set the bowl set over hot water to keep sauce warm, whisking occasionally, until ready to serve.

Recipes: MARIJUANA EDIBLES

Serving	6

Marijuana Spinach

INGREDIENTS

1. 1 tablespoon Marijuana butter
2. 1 tablespoon pine nuts
3. 2 bunches fresh spinach
4. 1 clove garlic, minced
5. 1 tablespoon sun dried tomato flakes (optional)

DIRECTIONS

❖ Heat to steam spinach, over medium low heat. Melt Marijuana butter in a pan, over medium heat and garlic, pine nuts, tomato flakes and stir well.

❖ Pour over spinach, mix slightly, and serve.

Recipes: MARIJUANA EDIBLES

Serving: 6

Marijuana Asparagus With Sesame Seeds

INGREDIENTS

1. 2½ lb asparagus, trimmed
2. 2 tablespoons Marijuana oil (or melted Marijuana butter)
3. 2 tablespoons minced shallots
4. 2 tablespoons sesame seeds, lightly toasted
5. 1 lemon
6. salt to taste

DIRECTIONS

- Preheat oven to 400°F.
- Toss asparagus completely coat with oil and place in an oven proof baking dish, and Bake for about 8 minutes, shaking the dish every 2 minutes. Add shallots and sesame seeds, shake the dish again, and keep baking a minute more.
- Transfer asparagus to heated serving bowl, season to taste with salt and squeeze lemon juice all over.

Recipes: MARIJUANA EDIBLES

Serving	4

Sauteed Marijuana Zucchini

INGREDIENTS

1. 2 teaspoons salt
2. 2 tablespoon Marijuana butter (or Marijuana oil)
3. 6 medium zucchini, washed and trimmed
4. juice of ½ lemon
5. freshly ground black pepper and salt to taste

DIRECTIONS

❖ Slice zucchini into thin matchstick like pieces (or use the small julienne disk of a food processor). Add salt and stir well to mix, and allow to stand for an hour.

❖ Rinse zucchini with water in a colander, and squeeze dry in a tea towel.

❖ Heat Marijuana butter, over medium low heat in a heavy skillet until melt. Raise heat to medium heat, zucchini and sauté for about minute. Remove to a serving dish, and season with lemon juice, pepper and salt.

Recipes: MARIJUANA EDIBLES

Serving 4

Marijuana Galic And Red Wine Filet Mignon

INGREDIENTS

1. 4 6 ounce filet mignon portions, each 2 inches thick
2. ¼ cup Marijuana oil
3. ¼ cup olive oil
4. 4 cloves garlic, thinly sliced
5. ¼ cup balsamic vinegar
6. 4 oz white mushrooms, thinly sliced
7. salt to taste
8. ½ bottle red wine (cabernet sauvignon)

DIRECTIONS

- Creating a small pocket, by slice into each filet lengthwise, stuff each pocket with the equivalent of 1 clove of garlic, and season filets with salt.
- Mix oils together and vinegar, and brush liberally over each filet.
- Heat olive oil in a large skillet over medium high heat. Sear filets for 2 minutes on each side. Remove filets from skillet, add mushrooms and cook for about 3 – 4 minutes, or until soft. Push mushrooms to the edges of the pan, and return filets. Add the wine, cover, and simmer for another 10 minutes for filets that are medium done.

Recipes: MARIJUANA EDIBLES

Serving 6

Marijuana chicken cordon bleu

INGREDIENTS

1. 2 tablespoons Marijuana butter
2. 6 skinless, boneless chicken breast halves
3. 6 slices Swiss cheese
4. 6 slices ham
5. 1 tablespoon cornstarch
6. 3 tablespoons all purpose flour
7. 1 teaspoon paprika
8. ½ cup dry white wine
9. 1 teaspoon chicken bouillon granules
10. 1 cup heavy whipping cream
11. 4 tablespoons regular butter

DIRECTIONS

❖ Pound chicken breasts if need. Place a cheese and ham slice on each breast within ½ inch of the edges. Fold edges of the chicken over the filling, and secure with toothpicks.

❖ Collect and mix flour and paprika together in a small bowl, coat chicken pieces.

❖ Collect butters in a large skillet, heat over medium high heat, for few seconds or until melt, add chicken and for 3 – 5 minutes or until browned on all sides.

❖ Add wine and bouillon. Reduce heat to low, cover, and simmer for another 30 minutes, or until chicken is no longer pink and juices run clear.

❖ Remove toothpicks, and transfer the breasts to a warm platter. Collect cornstarch with cream in a small bowl and blend well. Whisk slowly into the skillet. Cook, stirring until thickened, and pour over the chicken. Serve warm.

Recipes: MARIJUANA EDIBLES

Serving: 6

Marijuana Grilled Swordfish

INGREDIENTS

1. 1½ lb swordfish steaks
2. ¼ cup béarnaise sauce
3. ¼ cup marijuana cilantro marinade

DIRECTIONS

- Cost both sides of the swordfish with Cilantro Marinade, with brush.
- Cover and marinate in the refrigerator for 1 – 24Hours.
- Grill or boil swordfish for about 5 – 10 minutes per side, depending on the thickness of the steaks. Be careful not to burn swordfish.

Recipes: MARIJUANA EDIBLES

Serving	2

Home Made High Hummus

INGREDIENTS

1. 1 (15.5 ounce) can garbanzo beans (chickpeas), drained
2. 2 tablespoons marijuana oil
3. $\frac{1}{3}$ cup pitted spanish manzanilla olives
4. 1 teaspoon minced garlic
5. place garbanzo
6. 1 ½ teaspoons chopped fresh basil
7. 1 teaspoon cilantro leaves
8. salt and pepper to taste

DIRECTIONS

❖ Collect olives, garlic and beans into a blender or food processor. Blend for few seconds. add Marijuana oil and lemon juice, season with basil, cilantro, salt, and pepper.

❖ Cover and keep blending until smooth. Hummus can be served immediately, or covered, and stored in the refrigerator until ready to use..

Recipes: MARIJUANA EDIBLES

Serving: 8

Black Bean Buds Hummus

INGREDIENTS

1. 1 clove garlic
2. 1 ½ tablespoons tahini
3. ¼ cup Marijuana Oil
4. 1 (15 ounce) can black beans drain and reserve liquid
5. 2 tablespoons lemon juice
6. ¾ teaspoon ground cumin
7. ¼ teaspoon cayenne pepper
8. 10 greek olives
9. ½ teaspoon salt

DIRECTIONS

- Collect garlic into blender and for few seconds until mince, add black beans, 2 tablespoons reserved liquid, ½ teaspoon cumin, ¼ cup cannabis oil, 2 tablespoons lemon juice, tahini, $1/8$ teaspoon cayenne pepper and ½ teaspoon salt, keep blending until smooth, scraping down the sides as needed.
- Add additional seasoning and liquid to taste. Garnish with paprika and Greek olives.

Recipes: MARIJUANA EDIBLES

Serving	8

Marijuana Cheezy Margherita Pizza

INGREDIENTS

1. ¼ cup Marijuana oil
2. 1 tablespoon minced garlic
3. 8 Roma tomatoes, sliced
4. 2 (12 inch) pre baked pizza crusts
5. 8 ounces shredded Mozzarella cheese
6. 4 ounces shredded Fontina cheese
7. ½ cup freshly grated Parmesan cheese
8. ½ cup crumbled feta cheese
9. 10 fresh basil leaves, washed, dried
10. ½ teaspoon sea salt

DIRECTIONS

❖ Collect and stir together garlic, Marijuana oil, and salt, toss with tomatoes, and allow to sit for about 15 minutes.

❖ Preheat oven to 400°F (200°C).

❖ Coat each pizza crust with some of the tomato marinade. Sprinkle the pizzas evenly with Mozzarella and Fontina cheeses. Arrange tomatoes overtop, then sprinkle with shredded basil, Parmesan, and feta cheese.

❖ Bake in preheated oven for about 10 minutes or until the cheese is bubbly and golden brown.

Recipes: MARIJUANA EDIBLES

Serving 8

Canni Butter

INGREDIENTS

1. ¼ oz. ground buds
2. ½ cup salted butter

DIRECTIONS

- Heat butter in saucepan, over mrdium heat, until melt, add buds, and allow simmer for about 45 minutes
- Strain into glass dish with a lid. Discard plants
- Use immediately or you can freeze or refrigerate.
- One pound is to 1 oz. buds. But simmer longer.

Recipes: MARIJUANA EDIBLES

Serving	4

Marijuana Strawberry Banana Pancakes

INGREDIENTS

1. 3 mashed banana's
2. 3 ⅓ tablespoons cannibutter
3. 1 ½ cup flour
4. 5 tablespoon sugar
5. 1 ½ teaspoon baking powder
6. 1 ½ cup almond milk
7. ½ teaspoon vanilla extract
8. 2 eggs
9. 1 pint sliced strawberries
10. salt and pepper to taste

DIRECTIONS

❖ Slice strawberries and mash and mix with 2 tablespoons sugar and allow to sit for about an hour
❖ Collect all remaining dry ingredient in a bowl and together
❖ In another separate bowl collect and mix wet ingredients and mashed bananas. Add dry ingredients to wet ingredients and mix both together, make is well mixed
❖ Use batter to make pancakes in traditional manner
❖ Serve and enjoy with canni butter and syrup of your choice.

Recipes: MARIJUANA EDIBLES

Serving: 2 – 4

Canni French Toast

INGREDIENTS

1. 4 eggs
2. 1 tablespoon vanilla extract
3. 1 French baguette
4. 1 ½ tablespoon Canni butter
5. 3 tablespoon canni butter
6. ¼ cup sugar
7. 3 tablespoon syrup
8. ½ teaspoon salt powdered sugar
9. 1 cup almond milk

DIRECTIONS

- Coat baking dish with butter and cut baguette crosswise into 8 slices inch into medium size mixing bowl cream butters until well combined and spread over slices
- Add slices into dish butter side up, whisk remaining ingredients in a mixing bowl and pour over slices in baking dish
- Bake at 350° in your oven for about 45 minutes and dust with powdered sugar before serving.

Recipes: MARIJUANA EDIBLES

Serving | **4**

Marijuana Coffee Cake

INGREDIENTS

1. ²/₃ cup brown sugar
2. 1 tablespoon flour
3. 2 teaspoons cinnamon
4. ¼ cup canni butter
5. 1 crushed pecans

Filling

6. 2 cup almond flour
7. ½ cup canni butter
8. 1 cup sugar
9. 2 eggs
10. 1 teaspoon baking powder
11. 1 cup sour cream
12. 1 teaspoon vanilla extract
13. ½ teaspoon baking soda
14. ¼ teaspoon salt

DIRECTIONS

❖ Preheat your oven to 350⁰
❖ **Start with crumb topping**: add cinnamon brown sugar, flour, together, add butter, make crumbs and set aside
❖ Cream canni butter and sugar add eggs and mix until fluffy.
❖ Collect and mix other dry ingredients in separate bowl, add both bowl togrther until well mixed, stir in sour cream.
❖ Pour batter in to greased cake pan and add crumbs over top
❖ Bake in preheat oven for about 45 minutes or done. allow to cool for about 10 minutes before serving.

Recipes: MARIJUANA EDIBLES

Serving 4

Marijuana Guacamole

INGREDIENTS

1. ½ cup diced onion
2. 3 avocados, peeled and mashed
3. lime juice
4. 1 teaspoon salt and pepper
5. 1 teaspoon minced garlic
6. 3 tablespoons fresh cilantro
7. 2 teaspoons crushed cannibas
8. 1 teaspoon THC oil
9. 2 tomatoes diced
10. 1 teaspoon cayenne pepper

DIRECTIONS

- Collect and mash first four ingredients together in a medium size bowl
- Mix together remaining ingredients, in another separate bowl, stir in cayenne pepper
- Allow to cool in fridge for about an hour and serve.

Recipes: MARIJUANA EDIBLES

Serving | **2 – 4**

Home Grown Marijuana Mashed Potatoes

INGREDIENTS

1. 1 stick cannibas butter
2. 4 potatoes peeled
3. 1 cup shredded cheddar cheese
4. 4 tablespoon minced garlic
5. ½ cup sour cream
6. THC oil
7. salt and pepper to taste

DIRECTIONS

❖ Heat oil in a pan, over medium heat, add minced garlic and sauté for few seconds then set aside

❖ Bake potatoes in aluminum foil for about 45 minutes in the oven

❖ Mask softened backed potatoes in the oven and add remaining ingredients and stir and serve.

Recipes: MARIJUANA EDIBLES

Serving 2 – 4

Marijuana Butternut Squash Soup

INGREDIENTS

1. 2 tablespoons parsley
2. 1 cup chopped carrots
3. 1 teaspoon thyme
4. 3 lbs. Butternut squash
5. 3 tablespoon cannabis butter
6. 1 diced onion
7. 1 cup chopped celery
8. 1 tablespoon chopped sage
9. 5 cup vegetable stock
10. 1 ½ tablespoons cannabutter
11. 1 ½ teasspoon salt

DIRECTIONS

- Peel and slice and peel seeds from squash, slice into cubed chunks and steal for around 35 – 45 minutes. Heat oil in skillet, over medium heat, add diced onion, celery and carrots and herbs and cook for about 20 minutes or until brown, stirring frequently.
- Add remaining ingredients and simmer for another 20 minutes.
- Collect a blrnder and blend for few seconds or until smooth return to heat and simmer and serve.

Recipes: MARIJUANA EDIBLES

Serving: 4

Marijuana Cinnamon Rolls

INGREDIENTS

1. ¼ teaspoon nutmeg
2. 3 cup whole wheat flour
3. 1 ½ tablespoon baking powder
4. ¾ cup coconut oil
5. ¾ teaspoon salt
6. $1/8$ tablespoon cinnamon
7. 1 banana
8. 1 cup THC milk
9. ½ teaspoon vanilla extract
10. 1 teaspoon apple cider vinegar
11. 2 tablespoon brown sugar

Icing

12. 1 teaspoon THC oil
13. $1/3$ cup powdered sugar
14. 3 tablepoons THC milk
15. $1/3$ cup vegan cream cheese
16. $1/8$ teaspoon vanilla extract

DIRECTIONS

- Preheat oven to 400⁰ and grease your baking dish
- Collect all dry ingredients into a mixing bowl and stir well until mixed. In another separate bowl collect all wet ingredients and Combine the two bowls
- Roll out your dough, pour cannibutter over dough, sprinkle sugar over buttered dough and add cinnamon, and create rolls
- Bake for about 20 – 25 minutes at 400⁰
- Make frosting while rolls are baking, and blend for a minute. Allow to cool for few minutes.
- serve and enjoy..

Recipes: MARIJUANA EDIBLES

Serving 4

Marijuana Sprinkie Brownies

INGREDIENTS

1. Canni bitter
2. 3 tablespoons water
3. ¾ teaspoon vanilla extract
4. 3 cup sugar
5. 1 graham cracker pie crust
6. 1.4 lbs. chocolate chips
7. 6 eggs
8. 1 cup flour
9. 1 tablespoon baking powder
10. 1 pkg. chocolate chips
11. 2 ½ oz. pretzels
12. ¾ teaspoon salt
13. 4 cup mini marshmallows
14. 1 cup butterscotch chips

DIRECTIONS

- Preheat your oven to 350° and line pan with parchment paper
- Heat butter and chocolate chips over broiler, in a pan until melted and smooth
- Collect remaining baking ingredients together inn a bowl and beat well. Pour batter into baking sheet and top with pretzels into batter, add crumbled graham cracker crust into batter
- Bake for about 5 – 35 minutes, add marshmallows and butterscotch and keep baking for another 5 minutes
- Remove from oven and allow to cool.

Recipes: MARIJUANA EDIBLES

Serving	4

Cannabis Crispy Treats

INGREDIENTS

1. ²/₃ of a stick of cannabutter
2. 1 x 10 ounce bag of regular or mini marshmallows
3. 6 cups of crispy rice cereal of your choice
4. 1 x 12 ounce package of butterscotch chips

DIRECTIONS

❖ Heat cannabutter in a large saucepan over medium low heat, until melted. Add marshmallows and mix until completely melted and then remove from heat.

❖ Immediately add cereal and stir until coated.

❖ Mix in the butterscotch chips. Place mixture into a greased 13 x 9 x 2 inch baking pan. Allow it chill until the mixture hardens a bit. Cut into 2 inch squares. Potency of the treats can be adjusted by cutting bigger squares (3 – inch suggested).

Recipes: MARIJUANA EDIBLES

Serving 4

Cannadian Canna Pecan Pie

INGREDIENTS

1. 3 tablespoons extra strong cannabutter,
2. ¾ cup corn syrup
3. ¾ cup brown sugar
4. 2 tablespoons flour
5. 3 beaten eggs
6. ½ cup of milk chocolate chips
7. 1 teaspoon of vanilla extract
8. 3 tablespoons bourbon liquor (whiskey)
9. 1½ cups of pecans
10. 1 x 9 inch unbaked pie shell

DIRECTIONS

- Preheat oven to 350°F.
- Heat cannabutter in a saucepan, over medium heat until melt.
- Collect eggs, brown sugar, corn syrup, vanilla and bourbon into a bpwl and mix together until they are well combined. Add melted cannabutter and stir well. Mix in your pecans and chocolate chips. Make sure you mix it well so they are evenly distributed throughout.
- Place mixture into 9 inch pie shell and bake at 350°F for about an hour. Remove pie from oven and allow to cool.

Recipes: MARIJUANA EDIBLES

Serving | **4**

Chocolate Nut Canna Bites

INGREDIENTS

1. 1 cup of unsalted roasted peanuts
2. 2½ cups milk chocolate chips
3. ½ cup cannabutter
4. ½ cup glazed cherries
5. 4 cups of large marshmallows cut in half
6. ½ cup toasted coconut

DIRECTIONS

❖ Grease aluminum baking pan with a tablespoon of cannabutter, set rest aside for further use.

❖ Place chocolate into a large microwave safe bowl and heat on medium heat for about 30 second intervals, stirring until melted.

❖ Add the remaining cannabutter with the melted chocolate. Microwave for another 15 seconds or until cannabutter is fully melted and stir into the chocolate. Stir until both are well mixed.

❖ Pour in marshmallows, coconut, peanuts and glazed cherries.

❖ Mix everything together and Pour into the baking pan and chill in fridge until firm.

❖ Now you are ready to cut your squares, and enjoy.

Recipes: MARIJUANA EDIBLES

Serving 2

Citrus Canna Bread

INGREDIENTS

1. 2 large eggs
2. 1 stick cannabutter
3. ½ cup milk
4. 1 ½ cups cane sugar
5. 1 ½ cups flour
6. ½ cups chopped walnuts
7. 1 juiced lemon (or ½ juiced orange)
8. 1 teaspoon lemon zest (again orange works great too)
9. 1 teaspoon baking powder
10. ½ teaspoon salt

DIRECTIONS

- Preheat your oven to 350°F.
- Mix flour, salt (or lemon salt) and baking powder, into small bowl mix well until blended thoroughly.
- In another larger separate bowl, mix cup sugar, softened cannabutter, eggs together. Add milk and flour bit by bit, stir well add flour, then milk and then flour. Blend thoroughly.
- Mix in lemon zest, followed by the walnuts nuts. Pour this mixture into a buttered and floured 9" x 5" baking pan and place in preheated oven of 350F for about an hour or until done. remove from oven and allow to cool for few minutes before you take it out of the pan.
- While bread is cooling, mix the remaining ½ cup cane sugar and the lemon juice (from one lemon) thoroughly, until it becomes a lightly syrupy consistency and use this as a glaze.
- Pour over the cooled bread and let it dry. Or if you can not wait any longer just cut a piece and dig in.

Recipes: MARIJUANA EDIBLES

Serving   **6**

Marijuana Pot Wings

INGREDIENTS

1. 25 chicken wings
2. 1 teaspoon garlic powder
3. 6 ounces of tomato sauce, canned will work
4. ½ cup red hot sauce like tabasco
5. 1 teaspoon chili powder
6. ½ cup of cannabutter, melted

DIRECTIONS

- ❖ Preheat your oven to 400°F.
- ❖ Place plain wings in the oven and bake them for about 25 minutes, or until cooked through to your liking.
- ❖ Heat cannabutter in microwave until melt, add and combine it with the hot sauce, the tomato sauce, the garlic and chili powder in your large bowl.
- ❖ Mix and toss the cooked wings in the sauce mixture, making sure to coat them relatively well and covering each wing with about the same amount of sauce.
- ❖ Return coated wings to your baking sheet. Reduce oven to 250°F and bake for another 20 minutes. take them out of the oven and allow them to cool for about 5 minutes
- ❖ Serve and enjoy.

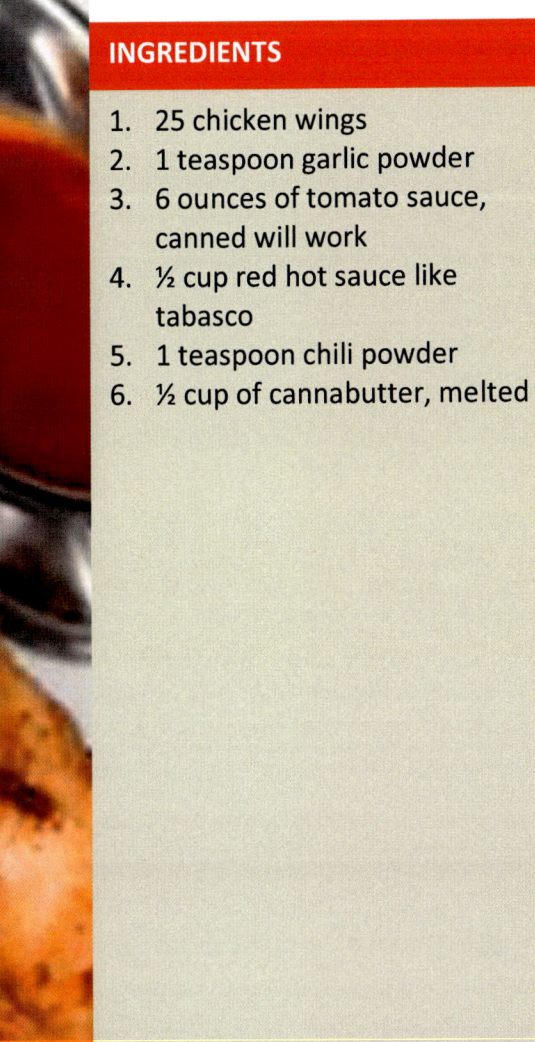

Recipes: MARIJUANA EDIBLES

Serving 4

Mary's Mashed Pot Potatoes

INGREDIENTS

1. 3 pounds Yukon Gold potatoes
2. 1 stick cannabutter in small pieces
3. 1 cup low sodium chicken broth
4. salt
5. 2 inches of pepper
6. 2 pinches of salt

DIRECTIONS

- Rinse under running cool water and peel your potatoes and place them into your large pot. add enough water so that the potatoes are covered my about 2 inches of it. Allow to boil over medium high heat.
- Once it starts to boil , reduce heat to medium low and simmer the potatoes uncovered for about 20 minutes or until potatoes tender and beginning to fall apart. At this point you can drain the potatoes in your colander and allow them chill for about 5 minutes.
- While they are chilling, collect broth and cannabutter in the pot you were using earlier, over medium heat, heat mixture until the butter is well melted and hot. Remove pot from heat and season the contents with freshly ground pepper and salt according to your personal taste.
- Take cooked potatoes and pass them through your potato ricer into the broth and butter mixture in the pot (or you can mash them first using a fork or masher and then reintroduce to the pot). Fold potatoes and broth and butter together gently until smooth, but do not overdo it.
- Add seasoning to taste.

Recipes: MARIJUANA EDIBLES

Serving **4**

Marijuana Bud Broccoli Cassarole

INGREDIENTS

1. ½ cup cannabutter
2. vegetable oil for greasing
3. Florets from 2 heads of fresh broccoli (chopped)
4. ½ cup of day old bread (cut into cubes)
5. 3 cups cooked rice
6. 1 cup chopped yellow onion
7. 1 pound of shredded cheddar cheese
8. 1 cup chopped celery
9. 3 cloves garlic, (finely chopped)
10. 1 cup baby portabella mushrooms, (sliced)
11. ¼ cup slivered almonds
12. 1 x 10.5 – ounce can of mushroom soup

DIRECTIONS

❖ Preheat oven to 350°F.
❖ Heat cannabutter in a skillet over medium heat, for few seconds or until melt, then remove and set aside.
❖ Grease a 9 x 13 inch baking pan with the vegetable oil.
❖ Mix broccoli, rice, onion, celery, almonds, cheese, mushrooms, garlic, and mushroom soup in a bowl and pour them all into the baking pan.
❖ Soak bread cubes in the butter, and then spread them over the entire mixture and bake for about 45 – 60 minutes, or until golden brown and bubbling. Take it out of the oven and serve.

Recipes: MARIJUANA EDIBLES

Serving 4

Marijuana Cheesy Macaroni N Treez

INGREDIENTS

1. ½ cup cold cannabutter
2. 1 tablespoon melted cannabutter
3. 1 cup flour
4. 2 teaspoons salt
5. ½ cup regular unsalted butter
6. 1 cup shredded cheddar cheese
7. ¼ teaspoon cayenne pepper
8. 1 teaspoon ground black pepper
9. 1 pound penne pasta
10. 1 cup shredded smoked mozzarella cheese
11. 1 cup shredded American or Swiss
12. cheese
13. ¾ cup grated parmesan cheese
14. ¼ cup breadcrumbs

DIRECTIONS

- Preheat your oven to 350°F.
- Cook penne noodles in a medium size pot, according to the label then drain and rinse under cold water and set aside.
- Heat cannabutter and butter together, in a large pot over medium heat, until melt. Add flour and whisk well for abouy 3 – 5 minutes while mixture is cooking, boil milk in another medium size pot, over high heat. Immediately after it starts to boil, slowly add heated milk to the butter flour mixture, whisking to incorporate. Add salt, black pepper, cayenne and keep cooking until mixture reaches a boil.
- Remove from heat, stir in the cooked penne and cheeses, saving ¼ cup parmesan cheese for the topping.
- Pour penne mixture into a greased 9 x 13 inch baking pan. Combine the breadcrumbs with remaining parmesan and 1 tablespoon melted cannabutter and sprinkle on top of the penne. Place in the oven and bake for about 30 – 40 minutes or until golden brown and bubbling. Remove from oven, allow to cool, serve and enjoy.

Recipes: MARIJUANA EDIBLES

Serving	4

Marijuana High Stir Fey

INGREDIENTS

1. 3 cups precut stir fry vegetables
2. 8 ounces rice noodles
3. 1 pork tenderloin (¾ pound cut into ¼ inch thick strips)
4. 3 tablespoons of cornstarch
5. 2 cups of fat free low sodium chicken broth
6. 4 teaspoons of cannabutter
7. 4 scallions, sliced (separate the green from the white parts)
8. 1 x 2 inch piece of ginger root (peeled and minced)
9. 2 cloves garlic, (minced)
10. lime zest from 1 lime (keep the lime wedges for later)
11. kosher salt
12. pepper (freshly ground recommended)

DIRECTIONS

❖ Cook noodles as label directs, then drain and rinse under cold water and set aside.
❖ Meanwhile, toss pork in a bowl ,with ¼ teaspoon of salt, pepper to taste, and 2 tablespoons of cornstarch.
❖ In another bowl whisk chicken broth and the remaining 1 tablespoon cornstarch.
❖ Heat a large nonstick skillet over medium high heat. Add 1 teaspoon of cannabutter cook untl melt, add pork and stir fry for about 5 minutes or until lightly browned. Transfer to a bowl.
❖ Add remaining 3 teaspoons of cannabutter to the skillet, then add the scallion whites, ginger and garlic. Reduce heat to medium low and cook, for about 2 minutes stirring occasionally.
❖ Stir in vegetables and 3 tablespoons water and keek cooking for another 4 minutes or until vegetables are crisp tender, , stirring occasionally. Add broth mixture to the pan and allow to boil and cook for another 5 minutes, stirring occasionally, until slightly thickened.
❖ Return pork to skillet along with the noodles, lime zest and a ¼ teaspoon salt and stir to heat through. Stir in scallion greens. Divide among bowls and serve with lime wedges.

Recipes: MARIJUANA EDIBLES

Serving: 2 dozen

Ganja Peanut Butter Cookies

INGREDIENTS

1. 1 cup cannabutter
2. 2½ cups of flour
3. 2 cups sugar
4. 1 cup brown sugar
5. 2 eggs
6. 1 teaspoon baking soda
7. 1 cup peanut butter
8. 1 teaspoon baking powder
9. 2 teaspoons vanilla extract

DIRECTIONS

- Preheat oven to 365°F.
- Place cannabutter in microwave and heat for about 35 – 50 seconds, or until melt and make sure not to boil it though.
- Mix melted cannabutter with 1 cup peanut butter and add ¼ cup flour. Add 1cup sugar, eggs, baking soda, brown sugar, baking powder and vanilla. Add remaining flour.
- Place remaining 1 cup of sugar in a separate bowl.
- Get spoon and mold the cookies into balls that can fit easily in the palm of your hand. Roll cookies in the sugar and put them on an ungreased cookie sheet.
- Place in the oven and bake for about 7 – 10 minutes.
- You can judge for yourself at this point if they need another minute or two, but do not over cook it much longer then that.
- Remove cookies from the hot sheet and transfer them to a cool plate and allow to cool for a minute or enjoy it hot.

Recipes: MARIJUANA EDIBLES

Serving 4

Late Night Marijuana Munchie Pancakes

INGREDIENTS

1. 1 ½ cup oats
2. 1 cup pecans
3. $\frac{1}{8}$ teaspoon vanilla extract
4. $\frac{1}{3}$ cup pumpkin puree
5. 1 teaspoon baking powder
6. ¼ teaspoon nutmeg
7. ½ teaspoon cinnamon
8. 1 tablespoon maple syrup
9. ¼ cup orange juice
10. ¾ cup THC milk
11. ½ teaspoon salt

Topping

12. 1 sliced banana
13. $\frac{1}{3}$ cup pecans
14. 1 teaspoon THC oil
15. $\frac{1}{8}$ teaspoon cinnamon

DIRECTIONS

❖ Collect and mix all first set of ingredients, mix well and heat skillet or griddle, heat, flip and serve
❖ Use toppings ingredients to garnish.

Recipes: MARIJUANA EDIBLES

Serving 4 – 6

Kidney Bean And Marijuana Mushroom Veggie Burger

INGREDIENTS

1. ½ onion
2. 2 medium carrots
3. 1 cup oats
4. ½ teaspoon garlic salt
5. 1 14 ounce can kidney beans, drained
6. ½ cup mushrooms
7. ½ red or yellow bell pepper
8. 1 egg
9. 2 tablespoons organic ketchup (optional as it adds sugar)
10. ¼ cup Marijuana oil

DIRECTIONS

- Collect carrot into food processor or blender and blend until grated, add oats and beans and keep blending for few seconds.
- Add remaining ingredients and process until well combined but still slightly coarse.
- Chill for at least 45 minutes then form into 4 – 6 patties.
- Cook these mushroom veggie burgers on the grill and add ¼ cup Marijuana oil.

Recipes: MARIJUANA EDIBLES

Serving | **4 – 6**

Black bean marijuana veggie burgers

INGREDIENTS

11. ½ onion
12. 2 medium carrots
13. 1 cup oats
14. ½ teaspoon garlic salt
15. 1 14 ounce can kidney beans, drained
16. ½ cup mushrooms
17. ½ red or yellow bell pepper
18. 1 egg
19. 2 tablespoons organic ketchup (optional as it adds sugar)
20. ¼ cup Marijuana oil

DIRECTIONS

❖ Collect carrot into food processor or blender and blend until grated, add oats and beans and keep blending for few seconds.
❖ Add remaining ingredients and process until well combined but still slightly coarse.
❖ Chill for at least 45 minutes then form into 4 – 6 patties.
❖ Cook these mushroom veggie burgers on the grill and add ¼ cup Marijuana oil.

Recipes: MARIJUANA EDIBLES

Serving: 4

Marijuana Chili Con Carne

INGREDIENTS

1. 2 chopped onions
2. 2 tablespoons cumin
3. 5 tablespoons canna butter
4. 30 oz. black eyed peas
5. 30 oz. kidney beans
6. 3 chopped tomatoes
7. 30 oz. black beans
8. 1.5 lbs. beef
9. 1/3 cup red wine
10. 3 tablespoons worcester sauce
11. 2 tablespoons chili powder
12. 2 tablespoon crushed red pepper or 1.5 teaspoon powdered cayenne

DIRECTIONS

- Place all beans and peas in a large pot of water over medium low heat.
- Cook until steam begins to form, then add wine, all spices and worcester sauce and keep cooking for about 30 – 45 minutes, add chopped tomatoes, onions, stirring occasionally.
- Add cooked beef and keep cooking for another 20 – 30 minutes, add cannabis butter and for about 2- 5 minutes.
- Serve and enjoy.

Recipes: MARIJUANA EDIBLES

Serving	1 cup

Marijuana Balsamic Vinaigrette

INGREDIENTS

1. ¾ cup extra virgin cannabis olive oil
2. ¾ cup balsamic vinegar
3. ½ teaspoon oregano
4. pinch of salt
5. Pinch of pepper
6. 2 finely minced cloves of garlic
7. 2 teaspoons dijon style mustard (optional)

DIRECTIONS

❖ Collect all ingredients into a blender and blend until thoroughly mixed. Store in mason jars in the refrigerator.

Recipes: MARIJUANA EDIBLES

Serving: 1 Loaf

Marijuana Meat Loaf

INGREDIENTS

1. 1 chopped tomato
2. 1 egg
3. 2 lbs. ground beef (or ground meat of your choice)
4. ½ oz. finely ground cannabis
5. 1 chopped stick celery
6. 1 finely chopped onion
7. 4 pieces toast (crumbled into bread crumbs)

DIRECTIONS

- Preheat oven to 375°F.
- Collect and mix all ingredients together in a large bowl. Make sure the meat you use has a decent amount of fat in it, as you will need it for the THC to be properly activated by the heat and absorbed by the fat and egg.
- Place newly formed meat dough in a meatloaf pan and bake in preheated oven for an hour or until the internal temperature has reached 160.

Recipes: MARIJUANA EDIBLES

Serving 4

Marijuana Spaghetti

INGREDIENTS

1. 1 package spaghetti
2. 1 tablespoon soy sauce
   parmesan cheese
3. 1/3 cup cannabis infused olive oil
4. 1 entire bulb garlic, chopped
   2 tablespoons vegetable oil
5. pepper and saltto taste

DIRECTIONS

❖ Boil water in a large pot, over medium high heat. Cook pasta to desired tenderness.
❖ While cooking, heat vegetable oil and soy sauce over medium heat, add chopped garlic sautee until tender.
❖ Reduce heat to low and add cannabis olive oil. Heat for about 5 minutes and then set aside. Toss pasta into the oil and mix in salt, pepper and parmesan cheese to taste.

Recipes: MARIJUANA EDIBLES

Serving 4

Marijuana Bake Salmon

INGREDIENTS

1. 1 thawed salmon fillet, 1 lb
2. 1 tomato, thinly sliced
3. 8 grams cannabis
4. 3 tablespoons dry bread crumbs
5. 2 cloves garlic, minced
6. 1 large onion, chopped
7. 1 teaspoon pepper
8. 1 tablespoon vegetable oil (Optional: replace with cannabis olive oil)

DIRECTIONS

- Grind up cannabis with a coffee grinder until it becomes a fine powder. Mix with dry bread crumbs and set aside.
- Spray a shallow baking pan with non stick coating. Place fish in the baking pan and sprinkle with oregano, garlic and pepper. Layer with tomato slices and onion. Mix bread crumbs with oil and put a coat on top of the fish. Bake at 350°F for about 12 – 15 minutes or just until fish flakes easily.

Recipes: MARIJUANA EDIBLES

Serving — **2 Loaf**

Marijuana Banana Bread

INGREDIENTS

1. 1 teaspoon vanilla
2. 2 bananas, sliced
3. 1 ½ cups a flour
4. ½ cup walnuts, chopped
5. ½ cup marijuana butter, soft
6. 1 cup sugar
7. 2 eggs
8. 1 teaspoon baking soda
9. ½ teaspoon salt
10. ½ cup sour cream

DIRECTIONS

- Collect melted marijuana butter and sugar in a bowl and mix well. Add eggs, vanilla, stir well to mix.
- Mix flour, baking soda and salt, stir into the marijuana butter mixture until soft.
- fold in the sour cream, walnuts and bananas. Spread evenly into the prepared pan.
- Bake at 175°C for about 60 minutes or until a toothpick inserted into the center of the loaf comes out clean. Then remove from heat and allow to cool loaf, in the pan for about 20 minutes.

Recipes: MARIJUANA EDIBLES

Serving | **2 Cups**

Marijuana Mayonnaise

INGREDIENTS

1. 1 teaspoon Fresh lemon juice
2. 1 teaspoon white vinegar
3. 2 or 3 Large egg yolks
4. 1 cup Marijuana Oil
5. ½ teaspoon Dijon mustard
6. 1 pinch sea salt

DIRECTIONS

- Collect and wisk egg yolks, lemon juice, salt, vinegar and mustard altogether.
- Add mixture to pot over medium heat, add oil gradually while keeping on whisking the blend. cannabis mayo will begin to thicken. In the event that it gets too thick, include a couple of drops of water.
- Cover mayo and chill. It ought to keep going for about a week in the cooler.

Recipes: MARIJUANA EDIBLES

Serving 4

Ganja Cheesecake

INGREDIENTS

1. 5 tablespoon Marijuana Oil
2. 1 cup graham cracker crumbs
3. 1 cup marijuana laced heavy cream
4. ¼ cup walnuts, chopped
5. 3 tablespoons brown sugar
6. 3 eggs
7. 1 tablespoon cinnamon, ground
8. ½ teaspoon ground nutmeg
9. 3 packages cream cheese
10. 1 cup white sugar
11. 1 cup sour cream
12. 3 tablespoons a flour
13. 1 tablespoon vanilla extract

DIRECTIONS

❖ Preheat oven to 175°C.
❖ Collect and mix well in a bowl crumbs, walnuts, brown sugar, graham cracker, cinnamon, melted butter and nutmeg, press into the bottom of spring form pan.
❖ Bake in pre heated oven for about 10 minutes. Remove from oven and allow to cool. Collect into a bowl cream cheese and sugar mix together until smooth. Beat in sour cream and heavy cream.
❖ Blend in the flour and vanilla. With mixer on low speed, add eggs one at a time. Pour batter over crust.
❖ Cook in pre heated oven for about 70 minutes. Refrigerate at least 6 hours or overnight before removing from pan.

Recipes: MARIJUANA EDIBLES

Serving: 2 Cups

Cannabis Butter

INGREDIENTS

1. 100g grinded Marijuana
2. 100g butter
3. 100 ml of water

DIRECTIONS

- Boil water over medium heat, in a pan add butter and keep boiling. Add grinded leaves or marijuana and stir it through the mixture.
- Allow to simmer for about 30 minutes. Pour mixture through a strainer to remove marijuana. Place pan in refrigerator so the butter will solidify at the top of the water.
- Discard water and marijuana butter is ready to use.

Recipes: MARIJUANA EDIBLES

Serving | **2 Cups**

Marijuana Milk

INGREDIENTS

1. 100 ml of milk or cream
2. 100 g grinded leaves or weed

DIRECTIONS

- ❖ Heat milk or cream in a pan, over medium low heat, but do not allow boil. Add leaves or weed and stir it gently. Keep mixture simmer for about 30 minutes do not allow to boil. Stir every now and then.
- ❖ Put milk through a strainer, to collect the and allow to cool down. Use your milk in milkshakes or ice cream.

Recipes: MARIJUANA EDIBLES

Serving: 2 Cups

Granola Infused With Marijuana

INGREDIENTS

1. 2 tablespoon honey
2. 1 tablespoon olive oil
3. 2 cup rolled oats
4. $1/3$ cup Canna butter
5. ½ cup almonds, chopped
6. $1/3$ cup dried cranberries
7. $1/3$ cup packed brown sugar

DIRECTIONS

- Heat oil in an expansive skillet over medium high heat, add oats, cook for about 5 minutes or until mixture beginning to cocoa and fresh. Remove from heat and spread out on a treat sheet to cool.
- In the same skillet, melt canna butter over medium heat. Add in nectar, cocoa sugar and keep cooking until bubbly.
- Return the oats to the skillet. Cook for 5 minutes more Pour out onto treat sheet and spread to cool.
- Once cool, exchange to an impenetrable compartment and add in almonds and dried cranberries.

Recipes: MARIJUANA EDIBLES

Serving	2 Cups

Marijuana Stoney Spaghetti Sauce

INGREDIENTS

1. ½ cup mushrooms, sliced
2. 1 can tomato paste
3. 2 tablespoons olive oil
4. ½ cup chopped onion
5. ½ cup marijuana, sliced
6. 1 dash pepper
7. 1 cup water
8. ½ clove garlic, minced
9. 1 bay leaf
10. 1 pinch thyme
11. ½ teaspoon salt
12. 1 cup black olives, chopped

DIRECTIONS

❖ Collect all ingredients in a pot, cover and simmer over medium low heat for about 2 hours or more stirring frequently. Serve.

Recipes: MARIJUANA EDIBLES

Serving | **2 Cups**

Marijuana Brownies With Walnuts

INGREDIENTS

1. 1 cup semisweet chocolate chips
2. 1 up marijuana butter
3. 1 tablespoon vanilla
4. 4 eggs
5. 1 ½ cup flour
6. 3 cup white sugar
7. 1 cup powder unsweetened cocoa
8. 1 teaspoon salt
9. 1 up chopped walnuts

DIRECTIONS

- Preheat oven to 175°. Lightly grease a baking dish.
- In a large bowl, mix together melted marijuana butter, sugar, and vanilla, beat in eggs and blend thoroughly.
- Sift together flour, cocoa powder, and salt. Mix flour mixture into the chocolate mixture gradually until blended. Stir in chocolate chips.
- Sprinkle batter evenly into the baking dish. Bake in preheated oven for about 40 minutes. Remove brownies from oven and allow to cool completely.

Recipes: MARIJUANA EDIBLES

Serving	2 Cups

Marijuana Tea

INGREDIENTS

1. 1 tea bag
2. 1 tea cup
3. 1 teaspoon of canna butter

DIRECTIONS

❖ Put tea bag and canna butter in the same cup. Boil water and pour it to and allow canna butter fully dissolve.
❖ Remove tea bag, add milk, and serve

Recipes: MARIJUANA EDIBLES

Serving 2

Marijuana Lobster Rolls

INGREDIENTS

1. ⅓ cup canna mayo
2. 1 tablespoon fresh lemon juice
3. ¼ cup celery, finely diced
4. 1 tablespoon fresh parsley
5. ½ tablespoon hot sauce
6. 1 tablespoon fresh diced scallions
7. 1 pound lobster meat, cooked and chopped
8. 4 rolls, split, toasted, and brushed with butter
9. salt and pepper

DIRECTIONS

- Collect canna mayo, lemon juice, celery, parsley, scallion, salt and pepper together and mix in a pan, add hot sauce.
- Add cooked lobster meat pieces to the Canna Mayo mixture. Toss lightly to cover the lobster meat with sauce.
- Fill toasted buns evenly with lobster salad.

Recipes: MARIJUANA EDIBLES

Serving	2

Marijuana Lifesaver Pizza

INGREDIENTS

1. 3 tablespoon marijuana, chopped
2. 1 onion, chopped
3. 1 pre made pizza base
4. 1 can tomatoes
5. 2 tablespoon olive oil
6. ¼ cup tomato sauce
7. 2 minced garlic cloves
8. 1 teaspoon chili flakes
9. 5 sliced hot Italian sausages
10. ¾ cup mozzarella cheese
11. 1 tablespoon chopped basil

DIRECTIONS

❖ Pre heat oven 180°C.
❖ Cook sausages in frying pan slice when cool, heat olive oil in frying pan, over medium heat, add onion and garlic cook for about 3 or until tender Spread tomato sauce on dough, sprinkle with your toppings
❖ Scatter sausage and mozzarella evenly over crust then put in oven and bake pizza for about 15 minutes.

Recipes: MARIJUANA EDIBLES

Serving: 4

Marijuana Knoll Guacamole

INGREDIENTS

1. 3 teaspoon marijuana, chopped
2. 1 fresh red chile
3. ½ cup onion, finely chopped
4. ½ cup limes juice
5. 1 tablespoon extra virgin olive oil
6. 3 large ripe avocados

DIRECTIONS

- Collec all all ingredients and mixed into a medium size bowl, except avocados and onion and set aside to rest for about 60 minutes.
- Put avocados and onion to the mixture and mashed up, using blender
- Until really smooth.

Recipes: MARIJUANA EDIBLES

Serving	4

Apple Pie With Marijuana

INGREDIENTS

1. $\frac{1}{3}$ cup chopped marijuana leaf
2. 4 cherries
3. 4 apple, cupped
4. ½ cup brown sugar
5. ¼ cup water
6. 2 tablespoons cinnamon

DIRECTIONS

❖ Pre heat oven to 175C.
❖ Collect marijuana into a blender and grind then mix in the sugar and water, mix apples with marijuana, sugar paste
❖ Sprinkle apples with cinnamon, and top with a cherry. cook for 20 minutes.

Recipes: MARIJUANA EDIBLES

Serving 4

Marijuana Pepper And Artichoke Dip

INGREDIENTS

1. 3 tablespoons mayonnaise
2. 1 jar roasted red peppers
3. 2 tablespoons potent cannabis butter
4. 2 jars marinated artichoke hearts
5. 1 leek, diced
6. ¾ cup grated parmesan cheese

DIRECTIONS

- Heat oven to 350°F.
- Drain and chop roasted red peppers and the artichoke hearts.
- Melt cannabis butter in a medium size saucepan, over medium low heat, add diced leek and saute for 2 minutes or until it becomes tender.
- Stir in artichoke hearts, parmesan cheese roasted red peppers, and mayonnaise. Place in an 8 inch glass round or square baking pan. Bake for about 30 minutes, or until the top of the dip is bubbly and lightly browned. Serve with warmed Marijuana Flat Bread or tortilla chips.

Recipes: MARIJUANA EDIBLES

Serving 4

Marijuana chili

INGREDIENTS

1. 1 oz. finely ground marijuana buds (use mid or low-grade buds if you don't want it to be too expensive)
2. 2 lbs. ground beef
3. 46 oz. tomato juice
4. 40 oz. tomato sauce
5. 2 cups onion (chopped)
6. ½ cup green bell pepper (chopped)
7. ½ cup celery (chopped)
8. ½ cup mushrooms (chopped)
9. ¼ cup chili powder
10. 2 cups beans of your choice
11. 3 cloves of garlic (minced)
12. ½ teaspoon oregano
13. ½ teaspoon sugar
14. ½ teaspoon cayenne pepper
15. 2 teaspoon cumin
16. 1 teaspoon salt
17. ½ teaspoon black pepper (ground)

DIRECTIONS

❖ Brown 2 pounds beef in pan or skillet over medium or medium high heat. Once is completely browned, drain thoroughly and set aside.

❖ Collect all ingredients in a large pot except for ground marijuana and allow to boil, for about 2 – 5 minutes. reduce heat to low medium and add in ground marijuana and keep cooking for 1 ½ – 2 hours, reducing the heat to low after an hour. Serve and enjoy.

Recipes: MARIJUANA EDIBLES

Serving 4

Marijuana Turkey Stuffing

INGREDIENTS

1. ½ cup chopped celery
2. 4 tablespoons (half stick) canna butter
3. ½ cup chopped wheat grass or chives
4. 5.25 cups rye bread crumbs (or any unseasoned bread crumbs)
5. 1 cup almonds, cashews (finely chopped)
6. ⅓ cup finely chopped onions
7. 2 tablespoons poultry seasoning (steak seasoning for duck)
8. 2 tablespoons red wine

DIRECTIONS

- Heat butter over medium low in a pan, until melt or in microwave on a low heat setting (this is to ensure that you do not compromise the potency.
- THC can survive temperatures up to 385°F). Once canna butter has been melted, mix all the ingredients together and stuff in the bird before cooking.

Recipes: MARIJUANA EDIBLES

Serving   4

Marijuana Crab Stuff Mushrooms

INGREDIENTS

1. 24 fresh whole mushrooms, small to medium size
2. 2 tablespoons cannabis butter
3. 1 teaspoon lemon juice
4. 3 tablespoons cannabis butter, melted
5. ¾ cup shredded pepper jack cheese
6. 1 green onion, minced
7. 1 cup cooked crab meat, diced
8. ½ cup soft bread crumbs
9. 1 egg, beaten with fork
10. ½ teaspoon dry dill weed
11. ¼ cup dry white wine
12. few leaves basil, cut into thin strips

DIRECTIONS

- ❖ Heat oven to 350°F.
- ❖ Pour 3 tablespoons melted butter into a 13 X 9 metal pan. Remove mushrooms stems and clean then set the caps aside.
- ❖ Chop up the remaining stems. Heat 2 tablespoons butter in a medium size saucepan, over medium heat until melt. Add onion and mushroom, cook together for about 3 minutes. Remove from heat and stir in the lemon juice, crab, soft bread crumbs, egg, dill weed and ¼ cup pepper jack cheese.
- ❖ Place mushroom caps into the baking pan, and mix them around until coated in the cannabis butter. Arrange the caps with the cavity side up, and stuff generously with the crab mixture. Top off with the remaining ½ cup of cheese, and pour the wine into the pan around the mushrooms (not on top).
- ❖ Bake for about 15 – 25 minutes, or until cheese is melted and slightly browned. Top with the sliced basil and enjoy.

Recipes: MARIJUANA EDIBLES

Serving 4

Marijuana Alfredo Pasta Sauce

INGREDIENTS

1. 1 cup heavy cream (use medicated milk recipe on cream for an even more potent sauce)
2. ¼ cup canna butter
3. 2 cloves garlic (minced)
4. 1 ½ cup fresh grated Parmesan or Gruyere cheese
5. ¼ cup freshly chopped parsley
6. oregano to taste

DIRECTIONS

- Heat canna butter in a saucepan over medium to low heat, until melt. Add heavy cream (hopefully medicated) and simmer on the same temperature for about 5 minutes.
- Add garlic, oregano, cheese and stir rapidly, keep cooking for about 5 minutes while leaving the temperature on medium to low.
- Stir in parsley and pour over your favorite pasta of a savory and medicated treat, just a minute before serving.

Recipes: MARIJUANA EDIBLES

Serving	4

Marijuana Potato And Olive Oil Soup

INGREDIENTS

1. 8 oz. medicated olive oil
2. 30 oz. water
3. 2 peeled and diced tomatoes
4. 8 chopped slices of bacon
5. 3 large peeled and chopped potatoes
6. 4 chopped garlic cloves
7. 10 peppercorns
8. 3 bay leaves
9. 1 large chopped yellow onion
10. salt to taste

DIRECTIONS

❖ Collect all ingredients (except potatoes) in large pot and heat for 15 minutes over 370°F. reduce to lower heat around 300°F – 325°F, cover and keep cooking for another 30 minutes, undisturbed. Then add chopped and peeled potatoes and keep cooking for another 45 minutes. When finished, you well have some very danky and tasty soup.

❖ Remove bay leaves after finished cooking the soup.

Recipes: MARIJUANA EDIBLES

Serving: 4

Marijuana Fried Butter Balls

INGREDIENTS

1. 1 cup seasoned bread crumbs (Italian seasoning seems to work best)
2. 1 cup flour
3. 2 sticks salted canna butter
4. ¼ cup cream cheese
5. 1 medium egg
6. peanut oil to deep fry balls in
7. Pepper and dill to taste

DIRECTIONS

- Mix together cream cheese, pepper, canna butter and dill, thoroughly in an electric mixer. If you do not have one, ensure you mix together thoroughly in bowl with a spoon.
- Make mixture into separate 1 inch balls, using either a small spoon or melon spoon, and place on a piece of wax paper on a baking sheet.
- Place in freezer and leave there until they are completely frozen. Once they are frozen, coat them in egg, then flour and bread crumbs. Place back in the freezer until frozen again.
- Once frozen, you can take them out and deep fry in peanut oil for about 15 seconds over 350°F. Drain on a paper towel. Enjoy, but be careful, just one or two of these will fully medicate you, even if your butter is of average potency.

Recipes: MARIJUANA EDIBLES

Serving	4

Marijuana Cilantro And Sun Dried Tomato Pesto

INGREDIENTS

1. 1 teaspoon brown sugar
2. $^1/_3$ cup medicated extra virgin olive oil
3. 1 clove of minced fresh garlic
4. 1 cup chopped fresh cilantro with or without stems
5. ½ cup sun dried tomatoes
6. 1 tablespoon finely chopped green chiles or fresh jalapeño
7. pepper and salt to taste

DIRECTIONS

❖ This not critical, but if time permits.
❖ Soak sun dried tomatoes in the olive oil for at least 2 hours.
❖ Once soaked, blend cilantro, chile or jalapeño, brown sugar olive oil, garlic and tomatoes until thoroughly mixed together. Take out, serve and enjoy. You can store it in the refrigerator for up to 2 days.

Recipes: MARIJUANA EDIBLES

Serving 4

Marijuana Chicken Pot Pie

INGREDIENTS

1. 1/3 cup cannabutter
2. 1 pound chicken breast, boneless and skinless and diced into cubes
3. 1/3 cup diced onion
4. 1 ¾ cup chicken broth or stock
5. 1 cup green peas
6. ½ cup diced celery
7. 2/3 cup 2% milk
8. 1/3 cup flour
9. 1 cup diced carrots
10. ¼ teaspoon celery seed
11. 2 9 inch unbaked pie crusts
12. ½ teaspoon salt
13. ¼ teaspoon crushed black pepper

DIRECTIONS

- Preheat oven to 385°F. (this is very important, any temperature over this will begin to diminish the cannabinoids).
- Collect chicken pieces, peas, celery and carrots. Add 1/3 cup water, cover and boil for about 15 minutes over medium high heat. Remove from heat and place in a strainer to drain.
- In the same pan, cook onions in butter (either cannabutter or regular butter) until they are soft and begin the become clear. Stir in pepper, salt, flour, and celery seed, subsequently stirring in the chicken broth and milk (for added potency use canna milk).
- Simmer this over medium low heat for about 10 – 15 or until concoction begins to thicken.
- Place the pieces of diced chicken in the pie crusts in separate pans. Pour the heated mixture that you just made over the chicken and into the pie crust and pan.
- Cover mixture with the alternate top crust and seal the edges, while trimming away and discarding excess dough. Use a butter knife to cut a half dozen slits in the top to allow moisture and steam to escape. Place in the preheated oven of 385°F for 40 – 45 minutes, or until the pie is golden brown on top. Take out and allow to cool for about 10 minutes before saving. Enjoy.

Recipes: MARIJUANA EDIBLES

Serving   4

Marijuana Tomato Basil Pasta

INGREDIENTS

1. 1 lb pasta, preferably spiral or bowtie
2. 4 roma tomatoes
3. 5 cloves garlic, minced
4. ¾ cup cannabis infused olive oil fresh basil
5. salt and pepper to taste

DIRECTIONS

❖ Cook the pasta according to the directions.
❖ While the water boils, prepare the sauce. Remove the seeds from the roma tomatoes and dice.
❖ Mince garlic, and chop the basil into a pan and mix together. Place pan over medium low heat. Add cannabis infused olive oil, salt and pepper and stir well. Remove from heat and combine in a separate bowl with the cooked pasta.

Recipes: MARIJUANA EDIBLES

Serving 6

Marijuana Grilled Macadamia Crusted Tuna With Papaya Salsa

INGREDIENTS

1. ¼ cup THC oil
2. ½ red onion, diced
3. 1 red bell pepper, diced
4. ¼ cup chopped fresh cilantro
5. 2 tablespoons lime juice
6. ¼ teaspoon hot chile paste, or to taste
7. 4 (6 ounce) tuna steaks
8. 2 cups diced papaya
9. 1 clove garlic, minced
10. 3 eggs
11. ½ cup chopped macadamia nuts
12. salt and pepper to taste

DIRECTIONS

- Collect onion, papaya, and red pepper mix together in a bowl. Add cilantro, lime juice, garlic, and hot chile paste. Toss well to combine, then refrigerate until ready to serve.
- Preheat an outdoor grill for high heat, and lightly oil grate.
- Brush tuna steaks with olive oil, then season with salt and pepper. Whisk eggs in a shallow bowl until smooth. Dip the tuna steaks in the egg, and allow excess egg to run off. Press into the macadamia nuts.
- Cook tuna steaks on the preheated grill for about 2 minutes per each side or to your desired degree of doneness, Serve with the papaya salsa.

Recipes: MARIJUANA EDIBLES

Serving	4

Marijuana Grilled Salmon

INGREDIENTS

1. $1/3$ cup brown sugar
2. 1 ½ pounds salmon
3. fillets lemon
4. salt to taste
5. $1/3$ cup soy sauce
6. $1/3$ cup water
7. ¼ cup THC oil
8. pepper to taste
9. garlic powder to taste

DIRECTIONS

❖ Season salmon fillets with lemon pepper, garlic powder, and salt.
❖ In a small bowl, stir together soy sauce, brown sugar, water, and vegetable oil until sugar is dissolved. Place fish in a large resealable plastic bag with the soy sauce mixture, seal, and turn to coat. Refrigerate for at least 2 hours.
❖ Preheat grill for medium heat.
❖ Lightly oil grill grate. Place salmon on the preheated grill, and discard marinade. Cook salmon for about 6 – 8 minutes per side, or until the fish flakes easily with a fork.

Recipes: MARIJUANA EDIBLES

Serving: 2

Marijuana Maple Salmon

INGREDIENTS

1. 1 pound salmon
2. ¼ cup maple syrup
3. 2 tablespoons soy sauce
4. 1 clove garlic, minced
5. ¼ teaspoon garlic salt
6. 2 tablespoons weed butter
7. $1/8$ teaspoon ground black pepper

DIRECTIONS

- Mix maple syrup, soy sauce, garlic, garlic salt, and pepper, in a small bowl.
- Place salmon in a shallow glass baking dish, and coat with the maple syrup mixture. Cover the dish, and marinate salmon in the refrigerator 30 minutes or more, turning once.
- Preheat oven to 400°F (200°C).
- Put baking dish in the preheated oven, and bake salmon uncovered for 20 minutes, or until easily flaked with a fork.
- Melt weed butter on salmon once finished cooking.

Recipes: MARIJUANA EDIBLES

Serving | **4**

Marijuana Fish Tacos

INGREDIENTS

1. 1 tomato, chopped
2. 2 pounds tilapia fillets
3. 2 tablespoons lime juice
4. 2 teaspoons salt
5. 1 teaspoon garlic powder
6. 1 teaspoon paprika cooking spray
7. 2 tablespoons of weed butter
8. ½ cup plain fat free yogurt
9. 1 ½ tablespoons chopped fresh cilantro
10. 1 ½ teaspoons canned chipotle peppers in adobo sauce
11. 16 (5 inch) corn tortillas
12. 2 tablespoons lime juice
13. 2 cups shredded cabbage
14. 1 cup shredded Monterey Jack cheese
15. 1 avocado peeled, pitted, and sliced
16. ½ cup salsa
17. 2 green onions, chopped
18. 1 teaspoon ground black pepper

DIRECTIONS

❖ Rub tilapia fillets with 2 tablespoons lime juice and season with salt, black pepper, garlic powder, and paprika. Spray both sides of each fillet with cooking spray. Preheat grill for medium

Recipes: MARIJUANA EDIBLES

Serving: 2

Marijuana Baked Tilapia

INGREDIENTS

1. 1 (16 ounce) package frozen cauliflower with broccoli and red pepper
2. 4 (4 ounce) fillets tilapia
3. ¼ teaspoon Old Bay Seasoning TM, or to taste
4. ½ teaspoon garlic salt, or to taste
5. 1 lemon, sliced
6. 2 teaspoons weed butter

DIRECTIONS

- Preheat the oven to 375°F (190°C).
- Grease 9 x 13 inch baking dish.
- Place tilapia fillets in the bottom of the baking dish and dot with weed butter. Season with Old Bay seasoning and garlic salt. Top each one with a slice or two of lemon.
- Arrange the frozen mixed vegetables around the fish, and season lightly with pepper and salt.
- Cover the dish and bake for about 25 – 30 minutes in the preheated oven, until vegetables are tender and fish flakes easily with a fork.

Recipes: MARIJUANA EDIBLES

Serving	4

Marijuana Hash Brown Casserole

INGREDIENTS

1. 2 tablespoons weed butter
2. 4 eggs
3. ½ package frozen hash browns
4. ¼ pound of your favorite cheese: shredded, grated, or thinly sliced
5. (Optional) Grits and salsa and or Tobasco, etc.

DIRECTIONS

❖ Add 2 tablespoons weed butter into a large skillet. Add hash browns, stirring so the oil coats most of them. Brown potatoes for about 6 – 10 minutes, stirring occasionally, until the bottom of the pile starts looking golden.

❖ Once potatoes are browned, beat eggs and slice or grate the cheese, if necessary. When the potatoes are light golden on the bottom, flip the potato patty over as cleanly as possible, and pour the eggs over the top.

❖ Allow side to brown for about 5 – 8 minutes or until eggs are mostly solidified. Now flip the mixture over again, as cleanly as possible, and then arrange the cheese in a thin layer on top. Cover the pan if possible and allow the cheese to melt, around 8 – 10 or less if covered. Serve with salsa and grits.

Recipes: MARIJUANA EDIBLES

Serving 1

Marijuana Reuben Sandwich

INGREDIENTS

1. 2 slices rye bread
2. 1 tablespoon weed butter, softened
3. 2 ounces thinly sliced corned beef
4. 2 ounces sauerkraut
5. 1 slice mozzarella cheese

DIRECTIONS

- Heat medium skillet over medium heat. Butter one side of a slice bread and place buttered side down, in skillet. Layer corned beef, sauerkraut and mozzarella on unbutteredside. Top with remaining slice of bread.
- Cook, turning once, until bread is browned, sandwich is heated through and cheese is melted. Serve and enjoy immediately.

Recipes: MARIJUANA EDIBLES

Serving	2

Marijuana Barbecued Beef Sandwiches

INGREDIENTS

1. ½ cup water
2. 2 tablespoons of weed butter
3. 3 pounds beef chuck
4. 2 onions, chopped
5. ½ cup distilled white vinegar
6. 3 tablespoons sugar
7. 1 (28 ounce) can diced tomatoes, with juice
8. $^1/_3$ (10 fluid ounce) bottle Worcestershire sauce salt and pepper to taste

DIRECTIONS

- ❖ Place roast in a Dutch oven, and sprinkle with chopped onions. Cover with tomatoes, water, sugar and Worcestershire sauce.
- ❖ Season with pepper and salt. Cook over medium heat with lid slightly ajar for about 3 hours.
- ❖ Remove meat, and shred with 2 forks. Discard bones, fat and gristle. place shredded meat back into sauce, and cook for 15 – 20 minutes or until liquid is reduced.
- ❖ Apply weed butter as desired

Recipes: MARIJUANA EDIBLES

Serving: 4

Marijuana Creamy Basil Chicken Pasta

INGREDIENTS

1. ½ cup breadcrumbs
2. 1 cup chopped fresh basil
3. 1 pound champanelle or gemelli noodles
4. 1 pound (about 2 large) boneless, skinless chicken breasts, cubed
5. ¼ cup weed oil
6. 6 – 8 cloves garlic, minced
7. 2 cups chicken broth
8. 1 ½ cups heavy cream
9. 2 – 3 cups finely shredded Fontina cheese
10. 1 teaspoon salt
11. ½ teaspoon pepper

DIRECTIONS

- Boil pasta per package directions. Drain (do not rinse) pour back into pot, add a tablespoon olive oil to it and cover to keep warm.
- As pasta is boiling chop chicken and place in zip top storage bag. Add breadcrumbs shake and use your hands to press crumbs into chicken until completely coated and most of the crumbs are no longer loose.
- Heat weed oil over medium heat in a large frying pan, add chicken and toss, for about 7 minutes, occasionally so that all sides get browned.
- Add garlic and toss. Try to toss this instead of 'stirring' it, this will help the breadcrumbs stay attached to the chicken. Keep cooking for another 3 minutes (check largest piece to make sure its done) and remove chicken from pan.
- If there is a ton of oil left in the pan pour most of it out, if not, add chicken broth, cream, salt and pepper. Allow to boil then add cheese, bring back to a boil and keep cooking, whisking occasionally for about 5 minutes.
- Add basil and boil, whisking occasionally, for another 5 minutes. Pour over pasta and stir until combined. Garnish with basil.

Recipes: MARIJUANA EDIBLES

Serving 4

Marijuana Garlic Basil Grilled Shrimp Pasta

INGREDIENTS

1. 1 ¼ cup weed oil
2. 2 tablespoons of lemon juice
3. 2 pounds shelled uncooked shrimp
4. 10 roma tomatoes.
5. Angel hair pasta
6. 3 tablespoons fresh basil
7. 1 tablespoon fresh oregeno
8. 6 cloves of garlic
9. 2 tablespoons fresh parsley
10. 2tablespoons white wine
11. 1 teaspoon salt
12. 1 teaspoon pepper

DIRECTIONS

For Shrimp And Marinade

❖ Chop 2 tablespoons fresh pareley, 3 cloves of garlic and 1 tablespoon fresh oregeno and place in a bowl.

❖ Add in ¾ cup olive oil, lemon juice, salt, pepper, white wine. Mix. Add in shrimp.

❖ Allow to marinade for three hours. Grill over low medium heat.

❖ **Sauce**

❖ Chop 3 cloves garlic, roma tomatoes and basil. Put chopped garlic, tomatoes and basil in a sauce pan. Add ½ cup of weed oil, add pepper, salt. Cook for about 5 minutes while stirring.

Combine

❖ Pour sauce on cooked angel hair and then add grilled shrimp.

Recipes: MARIJUANA EDIBLES

Serving 2

Marijuana Bloody Mari

INGREDIENTS

1. 2 oz. Marijuana Vodka
2. tobasco sauce to taste
3. 4 oz. tomato juice
4. 1 tablespoon lime juice
5. Pepper to taste
6. Ice
7. 1 tablespoon worcestershire sauce

To garnish

8. celery stalk, green olives

DIRECTIONS

- Collect mix ice, Marijuana Vodka, worcestershire sauce, tomato juice, pepper, lime juice and tobasco in a cocktail shaker. Shake for about ten seconds and pour into a tall glass.
- Garnish with olives and celery stalk.
- Please drink legally according to your local laws, and responsibly. Enjoy.

Recipes: MARIJUANA EDIBLES

Serving	2

Marijuana Screwdriver

INGREDIENTS

1. 5 oz. fresh squeezed orange
2. 2 oz. marijuana vodka
3. juice ice
4. lemon wedge

DIRECTIONS

❖ Place ice into a cocktail shaker. Squeeze lemon wedge over the ice and put it inside the shaker. Add marijuana vodka and orange juice.

❖ Cap and shake for about ten seconds or until mixed, and pour entire contents into a tall glass. Please drink legally according to your local laws, and responsibly. Enjoy.

Recipes: MARIJUANA EDIBLES

Serving 2

Marijuana Jello shots

INGREDIENTS

1. 6 oz. Jello mix
2. 10 oz. marijuana vodka (green dragon)
3. 16 oz. boiling water
4. 6 oz. cold water

DIRECTIONS

- Boil larger amount of water to a rolling boil, subsequently adding the Jello mix to the boiling water.
- Once Jello has dissolved, turn off the heat. add 6 oz. cold water (to cool it down) and then add the 10.oz of MJ vodka after the cold water. Pour into shot glasses or small plastic cups and refrigerate for about 3 – 5 hours, depending on temperature of the refrigerator.

Recipes: MARIJUANA EDIBLES

Serving 2

Marijuana Iced Coffee

INGREDIENTS

1. 1 teaspoon sugar
2. 6 oz Canna Milk
3. 2 teaspoons instant coffee mix
4. 3 tablespoons warm water

DIRECTIONS

❖ Collect together in a jar, warm water, instant coffee and sugar. Cover with lid and shake until the mixture is foamy.
❖ Pour into a tall glass filled with ice, then add the Canna Milk and stir.
❖ Add more sugar or some chocolate syrup if desired.

Recipes: MARIJUANA EDIBLES

Serving: 18 muffins

Marijuana Cupcakes

INGREDIENTS

1. ¾ cup milk
2. 1 ¼ cups flour
3. ½ – ¾ cup sugar (depending upon sweetness desired)
4. ½ teaspoon vanilla
5. 1 ¾ teaspoons baking powder
6. ¼ teaspoon salt
7. 1/3 cup weed butter
8. 1 egg, beaten
9. 1/3 cup chopped unblanched almonds, toasted
10. 2/3 cup blueberries (or whatever you wish to use)

DIRECTIONS

- Preheat to 350°F.
- Collect all dry ingredients together to mix well, in a small bowl.
- Cut in the butter until mixture resembles coarse crumbs. Whisk egg vigorously to incorporate air and make eggs light.
- Stir in egg, milk and vanilla and mix well thoroughly.
- Add to dry mixture and stir together (some lumps should remain) and add the blueberries.
- Fill in well greased muffin tins with batter until two thirds full.
- Bake in a preheated 350°F oven for about 20 minutes.

Recipes: MARIJUANA EDIBLES

Serving 4

Marijuana Apple Pecan Galaxy Cake

INGREDIENTS

1. ¼ teaspoon cinnamon
2. 1 cup flour
3. 1 egg
4. ½ cup whole wheat flour
5. ½ teaspoon baking soda
6. ½ teaspoon nutmeg
7. ²/₃ cup cannabis infused olive oil
8. ½ teaspoon salt
9. 1 cup granulated sugar
10. ½ cup pecans, chopped
11. 15 pecan halves
12. 1 ½ granny smith apples, peeled and grated
13. 1 gala apple, thinly sliced

For the glaze

14. 2 teaspoons cannabis infused olive oil
15. 2 teaspoons water
16. ¼ cup brown sugar

DIRECTIONS

❖ Heat oven to 325°F. Lightly coat a 9 inch spring form pan with nonstick cooking spray.

❖ Collect and mix together cinnamon, flours, baking soda, nutmeg, salt in a medium bowl until well blended. In another large bowl, whisk egg and sugar with ²/₃ cup cannabis infused olive oil.

❖ Stir flour mixture into the egg mixture, and add the chopped pecans and grated apples. Scrape into the prepared pan and flatten the top with a spatula. Arrange the apples slices on top of the edge of the cake, and arrange the pecan halves in one layer in the center.

❖ Make glaze in a small microwavable bowl. Mix together brown sugar and 2 teaspoons olive oil and water, and microwave in 30 second intervals until the brown sugar is melted. Brush the apples and pecans with half of the glaze and save the rest.

❖ Bake in the center of oven until a toothpick inserted into the middle of cake comes out clean, about 45 minutes. Remove from oven and brush the top of the warm cake with the rest of the glaze. Remove the ring by running a knife around the outside of the cake . Gently remove cake from base. Serve with a scoop of vanilla ice cream.

Recipes: MARIJUANA EDIBLES

Serving: 6

Canna Creamy Potato Salad

INGREDIENTS

1. ½ cup mayonnaise
2. 5 red potatoes
3. 5 Yukon Gold potatoes
4. 2 small sweet pickles, finely chopped
5. 2 tablespoons Marijuana butter
6. ½ cup prepared mustard
7. ½ cup sour cream
8. 1 stalk celery, finely chopped
9. 1 red onion, finely diced
10. 1 green bell pepper, chopped
11. salt and pepper to taste

DIRECTIONS

- Peel potatoes and cube, put potatoes in a large saucepan and cover with water. Cook over medium heat until potatoes are tender.
- Drain and set aside the cooked potatoes in a large bowl.
- Mash potatoes with Marijuana butter and salt and pepper to taste. Once mashed stir in the mayonnaise, mustard and sour cream, mixing well. Stir in celery, onion, green pepper, pickles. Serve warm or at room temperature.

Recipes: MARIJUANA EDIBLES

Ganja Garlic Mashed Potatoes

Serving 8

INGREDIENTS

1. 1 medium head garlic
2. 1 tablespoon olive oil
3. 2 pounds russet potatoes, peeled and quartered
4. 4 tablespoons Marijuana butter, softened
5. ½ cup milk
6. salt and pepper to taste

DIRECTIONS

- Preheat oven to 350 degrees F (175°C).
- Drizzle garlic with olive oil, then wrap in aluminum foil. Bake in preheated oven for an hour.
- Heat large pot of salted water, over medium heat, until boil. Add potatoes, and cook for 15 minutes or until tender. Drain, cool and chop. Stir in Marijuana butter, milk, salt and pepper.
- Remove the garlic from the oven, and cut in half. Squeeze softened cloves into the potatoes. Blend potatoes with an electric mixer until desired consistency is achieved.

Recipes: MARIJUANA EDIBLES

Serving: 6

Sativa Shrimp Burritos

INGREDIENTS

1. 2 tablespoons Marijuana oil
2. 12 ounces frozen cooked shrimp without tails, thawed
3. 2 teaspoons minced garlic
4. ½ cup plain yogurt
5. ½ cup mayonnaise
6. ½ cup chopped onion
7. ¾ cup long grain white rice
8. ½ cup canned diced tomatoes
9. 1 (16 ounce) can refried beans
10. ¾ teaspoon garlic salt
11. ½ teaspoon ground black pepper
12. 2 teaspoons pureed chipotle peppers in adobo sauce
13. 6 (10 inch) flour tortillas, warmed
14. 3 cups shredded Cheddar cheese
15. 1/3 cup salsa
16. ¾ teaspoon cumin
17. ¾ teaspoon garlic salt
18. 1 ½ cups chicken broth

DIRECTIONS

- Heat Marijuana oil in a saucepan over medium heat. Add onion, and cook until tender, stirring frequently. Stir in rice, and season with cumin and ¾ teaspoon garlic salt. Cook and stir until the rice is lightly toasted, about 5 minutes. Pour in chicken broth and the diced tomatoes. Allow to to boil, then cover and cook over low heat for 15 – 20 minutes, or until all liquid has been absorbed.
- In a small saucepan, stir together refried beans, ¾ teaspoon garlic salt, and black pepper. Cook over low heat, stirring occasionally until heated through.
- Place shrimp in a bowl, and stir in garlic until shrimp is coated. Heat a skillet over medium high heat, and coat with cooking spray. Saute shrimp until heated through and lightly browned.
- In a small bowl, stir together the yogurt, mayonnaise, and chipotle peppers until smooth. Refrigerate until ready to use.
- Place about ¼ cup of cheese onto each warm tortilla. Then place about ½ cup shrimp on the cheese. Top with ¼ cup beans, and ¼ cup of rice. Spread on about a tablespoon of the chipotle sauce, and salsa to taste. Roll up, and serve.

Recipes: MARIJUANA EDIBLES

Serving	6

Canna Cajun Seafood Pasta

INGREDIENTS

1. 1 pound dry fettuccine pasta
2. ¼ cup Marijuana Oil
3. 2 cups heavy whipping cream
4. 1 tablespoon chopped fresh basil
5. 1 tablespoon chopped fresh thyme
6. 2 teaspoons ground black pepper
7. 1 ½ teaspoons crushed red pepper flakes
8. 2 teaspoons salt
9. 1 teaspoon ground white pepper
10. 1 cup chopped green onions
11. 1 cup chopped parsley
12. ½ pound shrimp, peeled and deveined
13. ½ pound scallops
14. ½ cup shredded Swiss cheese
15. ½ cup grated Parmesan cheese

DIRECTIONS

❖ Cook pasta in a large pot of boiling salted water, over medium heat for about 7 – 12 minutes, or package directions.

❖ While, cooking pour cream into large skillet, and add Marijuana oil. Cook over medium heat, stirring constantly, until just about boiling. Reduce heat, and add herbs, salt, peppers, onions, and parsley. Simmer 7 to 8 minutes, or until thickened.

❖ Stir in seafood, cooking until shrimp is no longer transparent. Stir in cheeses, blending well.

❖ Drain pasta. Serve sauce over noodles.

Recipes: MARIJUANA EDIBLES

Serving: 6

Mexican Marijuana Chicken Corn Chowder

INGREDIENTS

1. 3 tablespoons Marijuana butter
2. 1 ½ pounds boneless skinless chicken breasts, cut into bite size pieces
3. 1 (4 ounce) can diced green chiles
4. ½ cup chopped onion
5. 1 clove garlic, minced
6. 2 cubes chicken bouillon
7. 1 cup hot water
8. 2 cups half and half cream
9. 2 cups shredded Monterey Jack cheese
10. 1 (14.75 ounce) can cream style corn
11. ¾ teaspoon ground cumin
12. 1 dash hot pepper sauce
13. 1 tomato, chopped

DIRECTIONS

- Brown chicken, onion, and garlic in butter, over medium high heat, using a Dutch oven, until chicken is no longer pink.
- Dissolve bouillon in hot water, pour into Dutch oven, and season with cumin. Allow to a boil. Reduce heat to low, cover, and simmer for another 5 minutes.
- Stir in cream, cheese, corn, chilies, and hot pepper sauce. Cook, stirring frequently, until the cheese is melted. Stir in chopped tomato. Garnish with cilantro.

Recipes: MARIJUANA EDIBLES

Serving	6

Marijuana Lasagna

INGREDIENTS

1. ¼ cup and 2 tablespoons chopped onion
2. 2 tablespoons Marijuana oil
3. ½ (16 ounce) package lasagna noodles
4. ¼ cup and 2 tablespoons chopped green bell pepper
5. ½ pound fresh mushrooms, sliced
6. 1 eggs
7. ¼ cup grated Parmesan cheese
8. ½ cloves garlic, minced
9. 1 (26 ounce) jar pasta sauce
10. ½ teaspoon dried basil
11. ½ (15 ounce) container part skim ricotta cheese
12. 2 cups shredded mozzarella cheese

DIRECTIONS

❖ Cook the lasagna noodles in a large pot of boiling water for 10 minutes, over medium high heat or until al dente. Rinse with cold water, and drain.

❖ Heat oil in a large saucepan, over medium heat, add mushrooms, green peppers, onion, and garlic and cook until onion translucent. Stir in pasta sauce and basil, allow to a boil. Reduce heat, and simmer 15 minutes.

❖ Mix together ricotta, 2 cups mozzarella cheese, and eggs.

❖ Preheat oven to 350°F (175°C). Spread 1 cup tomato sauce into the bottom of a greased 9x13 inch baking dish. Layer ½ each, lasagna noodles, ricotta mix, sauce, and Parmesan cheese. Repeat layering, and top with remaining 2 cups mozzarella cheese.

❖ Bake, uncovered, for 40 minutes. Let stand 15 minutes before serving.

Recipes: MARIJUANA EDIBLES

Serving 4

Marijuana Mac N' Cheese

INGREDIENTS

1. ¼ cup Marijuana butter
2. 8 ounces uncooked elbow macaroni
3. ½ cup grated Parmesan cheese
4. ½ cup bread crumbs
5. 2 cups shredded sharp Cheddar cheese
6. 1 pinch paprika
7. 3 cups milk
8. 2 ½ tablespoons all purpose flour
9. 2 tablespoons butter

DIRECTIONS

- Cook macaroni according to the package directions. Drain and set aside.
- Heat Marijuana butter in a saucepan, over medium heat, until melt. Stir in enough flour to make a roux. Add milk to roux lowly, stirring constantly. Stir in cheeses, and cook over low heat until cheese is melted and the sauce is a little thick. Put macaroni in large casserole dish, and pour sauce over macaroni. Stir well.
- Melt butter or margarine in a skillet over medium heat. Add breadcrumbs and brown. Spread over the macaroni and cheese to cover. Sprinkle with a little paprika.
- Bake at 350°F (175°C) for 30 minutes. Serve.

Recipes: MARIJUANA EDIBLES

Serving	4

Marijuana Scrambler

INGREDIENTS

1. 1 cup milk
2. 8 eggs
3. 2 tablespoon Marijuana Butter
4. ¾ teaspoon salt

DIRECTIONS

❖ Preheat the oven to 350°F. add Marijuana butter into a glass 9 x 13 inch baking dish.
❖ Collect and whisk eggs and salt together in a large bowl, until well blended.
❖ Gradually whisk in milk. Pour egg mixture into the baking dish. Bake uncovered for about 10 minutes, stir, and bake again for another 10 – 15 minutes, or until eggs are set.
❖ Serve and enjoy immediately.

Recipes: MARIJUANA EDIBLES

Serving: 4

Marijuana Flat Bread

INGREDIENTS

1. ½ teaspoon salt
2. 1 ½ tablespoons cannabis infused olive oil
3. ½ cup cold water
4. 1 ½ cup flour

Optional: Choose one of the following:
Cracked black pepper, parmesan cheese, shredded cheddar, sea salt, cheese, sesame seeds.

DIRECTIONS

- Heat your oven to 350°F.
- If using food processor, put salt and flour into the bowl and mix in the water and oil, process until the dough comes together. If using hand. Flour a clean surface in your kitchen and knead the dough for about 2 minutes. Cover the dough and put it in the fridge for at least a few hours, ideally overnight.
- Take dough out and separate into two equal size balls. Roll them out to $1/8$ of an inch thickness, keeping the round shape. Using a round pan like a pizza sheet, sprinkle a little flour or cornmeal onto the pan and put the dough on it.
- You can choose to add your toppings now, sprinkle a thin layer of cheese or sea salt onto the dough. Transfer the dough onto the baking stone in the oven. Bake for 8 – 10 minutes, or until desired crispness.
- If you do not have a baking stone you can use a pizza sheet, just make sure to check the bread frequently to keep from burning.

Recipes: MARIJUANA EDIBLES

Serving 2

Marijuana Tiramisu Milk Shake

INGREDIENTS

1. 5 oz. canna milk
2. 3 scoops vanilla ice cream
3. 2 oz. espresso or very strong coffee
4. 1 tablespoon cream cheese
5. Powdered chocolate
6. Whipped cream (medicated whipped cream works too)

DIRECTIONS

❖ Collect 2 ounces of espresso in a blender, pouring in 5 ounces of canna milk. Add cream cheese, as well as the ice cream and blend until the consistency is smooth.

❖ Fill in tall glass about $1/3$ full, then layer with some whipped cream, a dusting of chocolate, followed the remaining blended mixture, more whipped cream and a final dusting of chocolate.

❖ Enjoy and remember that this is going to medicate you fully, due to the amount of canna milk, so plan on relaxing or sleeping. Great treat after dinner.

Recipes: MARIJUANA EDIBLES

Serving 4

Marijuana Cinnamon Coffee Cake

INGREDIENTS

Cake
1. 1 ¼ cups flour (cannabis flour for extra potency)
2. ¼ cup canna butter
3. ½ cup sugar
4. ¼ cup sour cream
5. $^1/_3$ cup canna milk (or regular milk)
6. 2 eggs beaten slightly
7. 2 teaspoons baking powder
8. 1 ½ teaspoon cinnamon

Topping
9. ¼ cup canna butter
10. $^1/_3$ cup flour
11. $^1/_3$ cup brown sugar
12. 1 teaspoon cinnamon

DIRECTIONS

- Preheat oven to 375°F.
- Collect together all ingredients for the cake batter in a large mixing bowl. Mix thoroughly mare sure is well mixed, pour batter onto an 8 or 9 inch greased or buttered baking pan.
- Collect and combine flour and brown sugar for the topping in a bowl another, mixing in the canna butter and cinnamon after.
- Mix until it becomes chunky and crumbly. Spread over the batter and bake for about 25 – 32 minutes.

Recipes: MARIJUANA EDIBLES

Serving	24 Cakes

Marijuana Red Velvet Cupcakes

INGREDIENTS

1. ½ cup canna butter
2. 1 teaspoon vanilla extract
3. 1 cup buttermilk
4. 1 fl. oz. red food coloring
5. 1 ½ teaspoon baking soda
6. 1 tablespoon white vinegar
7. $^1/_3$ cup cocoa powder
8. 1 teaspoon salt
9. 2 eggs
10. 2 cups flour

DIRECTIONS

❖ Preheat oven to 350°F.
❖ Grease two 12 cup cupcake sheets with butter or canna butter.
❖ Mix softened butter and sugar in a mixing bowl, until is fairly fluffy, mix in buttermilk, eggs, food coloring and vanilla extract. Stir in baking soda and white vinegar.
❖ In another separate bowl, mix flour, sugar and salt together and begin to mix into the batter, mix thoroughly until blended, put batter in the greased cups and bake for about 20 – 25 minutes.
❖ Allow to cool on a rack and add frosting if desired. Serve and Enjoy.

Recipes: MARIJUANA EDIBLES

Serving 2

Marijuana Sloppy Joe Sandwiches

INGREDIENTS

1. ²/₃ cup cannabis infused olive oil
2. ½ cup water
3. 2 teaspoon minced onion
4. 2 tablespoons soy sauce
5. ¼ cup white sugar
6. 1 tablespoon brown sugar
7. 1 tablespoon red wine vinegar
8. 1 ¹/₃ cup ketchup
9. 1 tablespoon prepared yellow mustard
10. 1 teaspoon salt
11. ¼ teaspoon ground black pepper
12. ¼ teaspoon paprika
13. 2 lbs ground beef
14. Hamburger buns

DIRECTIONS

- Collect and mix together ketchup, water, white sugar, cannabis infused olive oil, brown sugar, vinegar, mustard, salt, pepper, and paprika in a large saucepan over low heat. Do not boil, but keep it warm.
- In another separate large saucepan, cook and stir the ground beef, onion and soy sauce over medium-high heat until the beef is browned and fully cooked.
- Drain the fat from the beef. Stir the beef into the warm sauce, and heat together on low heat for 10 minutes. Scoop onto toasted buns and enjoy with your favorite toppings.

Recipes: MARIJUANA EDIBLES

Serving 2

Marijuana Lemon Bread

INGREDIENTS

1. 6 tablespoons canna butter
2. ½ cups flour
3. 1 juiced lemon
4. 1 cup cane sugar
5. 2 large eggs
6. ½ cup milk (canna milk works too)
7. ½ cup cane sugar (again)
8. ½ cup chopped walnuts (optional)
9. 1 teaspoon baking powder
10. ½ teaspoon salt (or lemon salt)
11. 1 teaspoon lemon zest (finely grated lemon peel)

DIRECTIONS

❖ Preheat oven to 350°F.
❖ Mix flour, salt (or lemon salt) and baking powder, until blended thoroughly, in a small bowl. In another separate but larger bowl, mix softened canna butter, eggs and cup of sugar together.
❖ Add milk (or canna milk) and flour, first adding milk, then flour, then milk and then flour. Blend this thoroughly as well.
❖ Add in the lemon zest and mix, then add in nuts and mix, if you choose to add them.
❖ Pour mixture into a buttered and floured 9 x 5 baking pan. Place in preheated oven for 60 minutes. Remove and allow to cool for few minutes in the pan. At the end of the baking time in the oven, mix remaining ½ cup cane sugar and the juice of the lemon. Make sure to mix thoroughly and use this as a glaze to pour over the cooled bread, if you choose

Recipes: MARIJUANA EDIBLES

Serving **2**

Marijuana Sugar Cookies

INGREDIENTS

1. 1 cup softened cannabis butter
2. 2.75 cups flour
3. 1 egg
4. ½ cups sugar
5. 1 teaspoon vanilla
6. 1 teaspoon baking soda

DIRECTIONS

❖ Preheat oven to 375°F.
❖ Mix flour, baking powder and baking soda, in a mixing bowl. In another separate but larger bowl, mix the softened butter and sugar until the consistency is smooth, add in egg and vanilla extract and mix.
❖ Slowly mix in flour, baking soda and baking powder, roll to dough into small balls and place on an unbuttered baking sheet, baking for 8 – 10 minutes

Made in the USA
Las Vegas, NV
29 March 2021